Bible Promises

JUMBLE™

CROSSWORDS

Christopher Hudson
with Anna Floit

TYNDALE HOUSE PUBLISHERS, INC.

CAROL STREAM, ILLINOIS

Visit Tyndale's exciting Web site at www.tyndale.com

TYNDALE, *New Living Translation*, *NLT*, the New Living Translation logo, and Tyndale's quill logo are registered trademarks of Tyndale House Publishers, Inc.

JUMBLE™ and © 2009 by Tribune Media Service, Inc. All rights reserved. Used by permission.

Bible Promises Jumble Crosswords

Designed by Mark Anthony Lane II

Produced with the assistance of Hudson & Associates. Special thanks are given to Megan Chrans.

ISBN 978-1-4143-2695-5

Printed in the United States of America

15 14 13 12 11 10 09
7   6   5   4   3   2   1

CONTENTS

JUMBLE CROSSWORDS

GOD SAVES CRUSHED SPIRITS

Complete the crossword puzzle by looking at the clues and unscrambling the answers. When the puzzle is complete, unscramble the circled letters to solve the Mystery Answer.

The LORD is close to the brokenhearted;
he rescues those whose spirits are
crushed.

PSALM 34:18

ACROSS

1	ELEVATION	HIGETH
5	LOGICAL	ILTONARA
6	MISTAKES	RORSER
7	CARNIVAL	LAFEVIST

DOWN

1	"SHE DID IT ALL BY _____."	RELFESH
2	CURIOSITY	TRISENET
3	CARES FOR	DENST
4	OBVIOUSLY	PLYLANI

MYSTERY ANSWER: " ⬚⬚⬚⬚ ⬚⬚⬚⬚⬚⬚⬚⬚⬚ "

CLUE: To those who are hurting, God is a _____ _____.

1

GOD HAS GOOD PURPOSES

Complete the crossword puzzle by looking at the clues and unscrambling the answers. When the puzzle is complete, unscramble the circled letters to solve the Mystery Answer.

It is God who works in you to will and to act according to his good purpose.
PHILIPPIANS 2:13, NIV

ACROSS

1	INFANTS	BISEBA
3	FRESHEN	WREEN
6	WEEK'S END	YUTSADAR
7	HIT	PHUNC

DOWN

1	SMILES BROADLY	MABES
2	EXPLODING	BIRNGUST
4	TRUE STAR	THORN
5	RICHES	HATLEW

MYSTERY ANSWER:

CLUE: God's work in our lives is _____.

GOD HEARS HIS PEOPLE

Complete the crossword puzzle by looking at the clues and unscrambling the answers. When the puzzle is complete, unscramble the circled letters to solve the Mystery Answer.

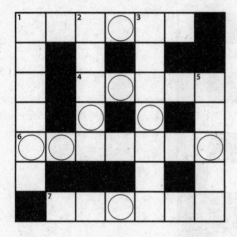

You hear, O LORD, the desire of the afflicted; you encourage them, and you listen to their cry.

PSALM 10:17, NIV

ACROSS

1	TYPE OF FRACTURE	S R E S T S
4	WIDE	D O A R B
6	FREESTYLE UNITS	L H S N G E T
7	IN A NICE MANNER	I D N Y L K

DOWN

1	PALLID OR WAN	S K Y C I L
2	SIGN OF SPRING	N O R B I
3	LIKE A LEOPARD'S COAT	D O P S T E T
5	POWDERY	D Y T S U

MYSTERY ANSWER:

CLUE: God is a good _____.

GOD IS THE GIVER OF LIFE

Complete the crossword puzzle by looking at the clues and unscrambling the answers. When the puzzle is complete, unscramble the circled letters to solve the Mystery Answer.

Each day the LORD pours his unfailing love upon me, and through each night I sing his songs, praying to God who gives me life.

PSALM 42:8

ACROSS

3	CHILL	REZFEE
5	ACCOMPLISHED	HAVIDECE
7	CREATES	GESSDIN
8	CORRODES	STURS

DOWN

1	HIRED HELP	STREVANS
2	REPAIRS	SNEMD
4	SHRIVELED GRAPES	ISSIRNA
6	CLOUDLESS	CAREL

MYSTERY ANSWER: ⬚⬚⬚⬚⬚⬚⬚⬚⬚⬚

CLUE: Our response to God's love.

4

GOD WILL RESTORE YOU

Complete the crossword puzzle by looking at the clues and unscrambling the answers. When the puzzle is complete, unscramble the circled letters to solve the Mystery Answer.

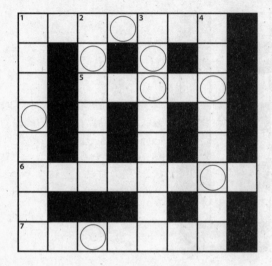

You have allowed me to suffer much hardship, but you will restore me to life again and lift me up from the depths of the earth.

PSALM 71:20

ACROSS

1	CORRUPT	D E O R O C K
5	NARROW WATERWAY	L A C N A
6	HOLD BACK	R I S T E N A R
7	SPREADS OUT	S L O P E D Y

DOWN

1	HOLLERED	O M A R C L E D
2	HAPPENS	C O R S U C
3	BOUNDING MARSUPIAL	G R A K O O N A
4	MARINE MAMMALS	S P I D L O H N

MYSTERY ANSWER:

CLUE: This psalmist does not _____ about his hardship.

5

GOD MAKES YOU MORE THAN CONQUERORS

Complete the crossword puzzle by looking at the clues and unscrambling the answers. When the puzzle is complete, unscramble the circled letters to solve the Mystery Answer.

No, despite all these things, overwhelming victory is ours through Christ, who loved us.

ROMANS 8:37

ACROSS

1	DISENTANGLING	GUNNITY
4	PURE	NEINNOCT
6	HEMISPHERE DIVIDER	QUETARO
7	ODORS	MESSLL

DOWN

1	COSMOS	ENISURVE
2	LANGUAGES	SEONTUG
3	MILITARY LEADER	GLEARNE
5	MUNICIPALITIES	ETISIC

MYSTERY ANSWER: ☐☐☐☐☐☐☐☐☐☐☐

CLUE: The Lord's conquering army is always _____.

6

GOD IS FAITHFUL

Complete the crossword puzzle by looking at the clues and unscrambling the answers. When the puzzle is complete, unscramble the circled letters to solve the Mystery Answer.

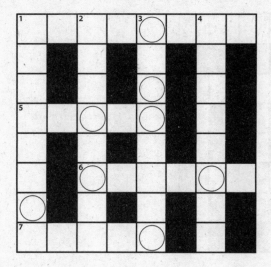

The LORD must wait for you to come to him so he can show you his love and compassion. For the LORD is a faithful God. Blessed are those who wait for his help.

ISAIAH 30:18

ACROSS

1 SAVAGELY — LERYFICE

5 KICK OUT — CIVET

6 PREPARES — MERSIP

7 EVADE — DEDOG

DOWN

1 ABOVE THE EYEBROWS — HOFEADER

2 PROVIDED WITH — PEPQUEDI

3 SORRY — TRONITEC

4 SLOTH — ZANISSEL

MYSTERY ANSWER:

CLUE: Virtue gained by waiting.

7

GOD GRANTS REQUESTS

Complete the crossword puzzle by looking at the clues and unscrambling the answers. When the puzzle is complete, unscramble the circled letters to solve the Mystery Answer.

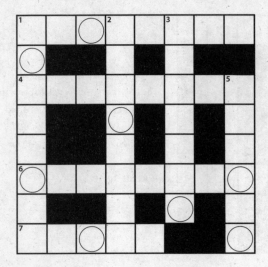

If you remain in me and my words remain in you, you may ask for anything you want, and it will be granted!
JOHN 15:7

ACROSS

1 AUTHENTIC   GIONARLI

4 MAYBE   LOBSISPY

6 TRAIN DRIVER   GENENIRE

7 CLOCKED   MEDIT

DOWN

1 ADVERSARY   PENNPOOT

2 FUEL   NOGSIALE

3 GENTLE BITES   BILBENS

5 LONGS   SNAREY

MYSTERY ANSWER:

CLUE: We can always trust God's _____.

8

GOD MAKES YOU CITIZENS OF HEAVEN

Complete the crossword puzzle by looking at the clues and unscrambling the answers. When the puzzle is complete, unscramble the circled letters to solve the Mystery Answer.

We are citizens of heaven, where the Lord Jesus Christ lives. And we are eagerly waiting for him to return as our Savior. He will take our weak mortal bodies and change them into glorious bodies like his own, using the same power with which he will bring everything under his control.

PHILIPPIANS 3:20-21

ACROSS

2	PENNANTS	GLAFS
5	UNINTERESTED	ODERB
6	COMPRESSES	SEZEQUES
7	TREE EXTENSIONS	BANSERCH

DOWN

1	OBLIGATIONS	STEBD
2	EQUATION	MUFALOR
3	VIEWERS	DEECUNIA
4	MATCHLESS	ERSPUME

MYSTERY ANSWER:

CLUE: What we'll be when Christ returns.

GOD REWARDS THOSE WHO PURSUE HIM

Complete the crossword puzzle by looking at the clues and unscrambling the answers. When the puzzle is complete, unscramble the circled letters to solve the Mystery Answer.

Whoever pursues righteousness and unfailing love will find life, righteousness, and honor.
PROVERBS 21:21

ACROSS

1	CITRUS FRUITS	GONEARS
5	CONFIDENTIAL	SLAPNEOR
6	PARAGRAPH ELEMENT	TEENSNEC
7	ABANDONED	REDETEDS

DOWN

1	DISAGREED	POPEDOS
2	SMOCK	PRANO
3	STUDY OF ANGLES	EMOTYGER
4	LOOKED FOR	HERSECAD

MYSTERY ANSWER:

CLUE: Try to live a life that is free from worldly _____.

GOD IS STEADFAST

Complete the crossword puzzle by looking at the clues and unscrambling the answers. When the puzzle is complete, unscramble the circled letters to solve the Mystery Answer.

To the faithful you show yourself faithful; to those with integrity you show integrity.

2 SAMUEL 22:26

ACROSS

1	ART OF GOVERNMENT	SILTOPIC
5	MONIKERS	MESAN
6	SUFFICIENT	TAQUADEE
7	FORTHRIGHT	ENSOTH

DOWN

1	BREAKFAST FOOD	ACKNAPSE
2	TWO-BY-FOURS	BULREM
3	THIN PAPER	SEUSIT
4	SALEM AND BOISE	TIPALSAC

MYSTERY ANSWER:

CLUE: The ways of the Lord are _____.

11

GOD WILL REIGN FOREVER

Complete the crossword puzzle by looking at the clues and unscrambling the answers. When the puzzle is complete, unscramble the circled letters to solve the Mystery Answer.

LORD, you remain the same forever!
Your throne continues from
generation to generation.
LAMENTATIONS 5:19

ACROSS

1	DECLINING	**G A L L N I F**
4	LOUD	**O I S Y N**
6	ALIKE	**L U E A Q**
7	APPEARS	**M E S S E**

DOWN

1	WOODEN BARRIER	**C E N E F**
2	FREE TIME	**S L E E R I U**
3	GOLIATHS	**T A S I N G**
5	EGG PARTS	**S Y K O L**

MYSTERY ANSWER:

CLUE: God is faithful to every _____.

12

GOD CAN MAKE YOU HIS CHILDREN

Complete the crossword puzzle by looking at the clues and unscrambling the answers. When the puzzle is complete, unscramble the circled letters to solve the Mystery Answer.

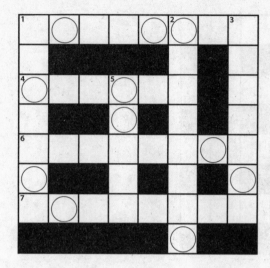

Blessed are the peacemakers, for they will be called sons of God.
MATTHEW 5:9, NIV

ACROSS

1	ORATORS	SEESPARK
4	ILLUSION	IRGAME
6	COLORFUL MAKEUP	PLIKCIST
7	ANXIOUS	SELTSERS

DOWN

1	COMPARABLE	MIRSAIL
2	MASCARA'S COMPANION	NEYELIER
3	SMITES	KESSIRT
5	ADVANTAGE	TASES

MYSTERY ANSWER:

CLUE: The sons of God will be _____.

GOD BLESSES SUBMISSION

Complete the crossword puzzle by looking at the clues and unscrambling the answers. When the puzzle is complete, unscramble the circled letters to solve the Mystery Answer.

Submit to God, and you will have peace; then things will go well for you.
JOB 22:21

ACROSS

1 INCORPORATED — **L U D D I N E C**

5 REBOUND — **O N C U B E**

6 SUFFICIENT — **A Q U T E E D A**

7 REVOLVING — **C R I N G I L C**

DOWN

1 EXAMPLE — **N I S C E T A N**

2 WIRE — **B L E A C**

3 UNCOMMON — **S U N U L A U**

4 THRILLING — **C I X I T G E N**

MYSTERY ANSWER:

CLUE: The Lord blesses those who follow his _____.

GOD WILL KEEP YOU IN HIS HANDS

Complete the crossword puzzle by looking at the clues and unscrambling the answers. When the puzzle is complete, unscramble the circled letters to solve the Mystery Answer.

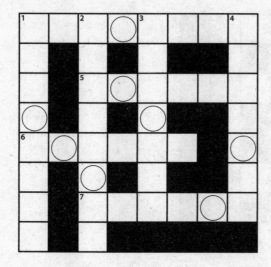

If I ride the wings of the morning, if I dwell by the farthest oceans, even there your hand will guide me, and your strength will support me.
PSALM 139:9-10

ACROSS

1 INHABITED   **C O U P D I E C**

5 CREATURE   **M A N A I L**

6 AID   **A S T I S S**

7 MORE QUICKLY   **T A F R E S**

DOWN

1 FUNCTIONED   **T E E P R O A D**

2 CATEGORIZE   **S L I S C A F Y**

3 CLERGYMEN   **S P I R S E T**

4 DISPENSE   **L E E D I R V**

MYSTERY ANSWER:

CLUE: In his hands, God holds the entire _____.

15

GOD GRANTS SAFE SLEEP

Complete the crossword puzzle by looking at the clues and unscrambling the answers. When the puzzle is complete, unscramble the circled letters to solve the Mystery Answer.

In peace I will lie down and sleep, for you alone, O LORD, will keep me safe.
PSALM 4:8

ACROSS

1	TYPE OF JAM	CAFRFIT
5	FISH TANK	RUQAIMAU
6	MANIPULATE	LONTORC
7	TUNE	DEMYOL

DOWN

1	DISASTROUS	GRITAC
2	FOIL AND CANS	INUMMULA
3	GROWER	ARRFEM
4	SNICKERED	CLUCHDEK

MYSTERY ANSWER:

CLUE: **The stillness of night.**

16

GOD PROVIDES SECURITY

Complete the crossword puzzle by looking at the clues and unscrambling the answers. When the puzzle is complete, unscramble the circled letters to solve the Mystery Answer.

Those who fear the LORD are secure; he will be a refuge for their children.

PROVERBS 14:26

ACROSS

1 SLICK   PLIESYRP

4 RADICAL   MEERTEX

6 FINISH   TECLOPEM

7 REBUKED   CODDELS

DOWN

1 BIOLOGY AND CHEMISTRY   CESSNIEC

2 CAST OFF   JECEDRET

3 SKINNED   DELEPE

5 BEAT   PEMOT

MYSTERY ANSWER:

CLUE: The Lord gives _____ to those who fear him.

GOD KEEPS YOU ON HIS MIND

Complete the crossword puzzle by looking at the clues and unscrambling the answers. When the puzzle is complete, unscramble the circled letters to solve the Mystery Answer.

How precious are your thoughts about me, O God. They cannot be numbered!

PSALM 139:17

ACROSS

1	TAPIOCA AND FIGGY	DUNDPIGS
4	REVEAL	CORNEVU
6	CHOSE	DEELTEC
7	EXHAUSTING	RIGNIT

DOWN

1	FELL	GLEDNUP
2	CERTIFICATE	NECTODUM
3	ORIGINATOR	ONNTRIVE
5	BLUSH	DERNED

MYSTERY ANSWER:

CLUE: Jehovah-jireh, God is our _____.

18

GOD WILL LOVINGLY LEAD YOU

Complete the crossword puzzle by looking at the clues and unscrambling the answers. When the puzzle is complete, unscramble the circled letters to solve the Mystery Answer.

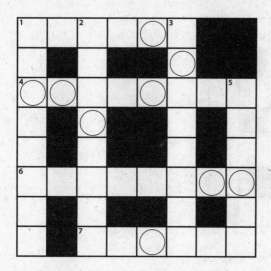

Even though I walk through the valley of the shadow of death, I will fear no evil, for you are with me; your rod and your staff, they comfort me.

PSALM 23:4, NIV

ACROSS

1	CINEMA	VOSEMI
4	HAIR CLEANSERS	SOPHOMSA
6	INCORPORATES	LINDSCUE
7	GRIEF	WROORS

DOWN

1	ITCHY PEST	QUITSOOM
2	BRIDGES	DAVITUSC
3	HIGHWAY BORDER	DHULEORS
5	PLAYGROUND RIDE	WESSAE

MYSTERY ANSWER:

CLUE: **Leads little lambs.**

19

GOD GIVES DIRECTION

Complete the crossword puzzle by looking at the clues and unscrambling the answers. When the puzzle is complete, unscramble the circled letters to solve the Mystery Answer.

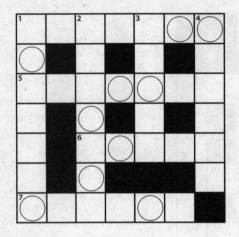

We can make our plans, but the LORD determines our steps.

PROVERBS 16:9

ACROSS

1	SETTING FOR A MUSICAL	R E E H A T T
5	INCHED	W E R D L A C
6	TOPIC OF DISCUSSION	U S I S E
7	AMOUNT	E R E D G E

DOWN

1	DELIGHTED	L E C K T I D
2	CLEANING THE SLATE	N E S G R I A
3	REPORTS	L E L T S
4	GROOVED	G R E D I D

MYSTERY ANSWER:

CLUE: Mount Sinai setting.

GOD HELPS US FLOURISH

Complete the crossword puzzle by looking at the clues and unscrambling the answers. When the puzzle is complete, unscramble the circled letters to solve the Mystery Answer.

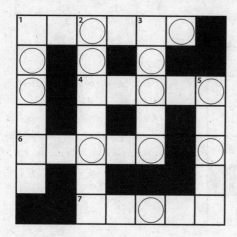

Whoever trusts in his riches will fall, but the righteous will thrive like a green leaf.

PROVERBS 11:28, NIV

ACROSS

1 CHARMING ONE   P I C N E R

4 LEAPS   M J U S P

6 SHADE OF PINK   C L O A R

7 AMBITION   V I D R E

DOWN

1 GUIDING PRINCIPLE   C O P I L Y

2 HURT   J U D R I N E

3 DESERT DWELLER   C L E A M

5 MALICE   P E T I S

MYSTERY ANSWER: ☐☐☐☐☐☐☐☐☐☐☐☐

CLUE: Without trust in God, even these people will stumble.

GOD COMPLETES HIS PERFECT WILL

Complete the crossword puzzle by looking at the clues and unscrambling the answers. When the puzzle is complete, unscramble the circled letters to solve the Mystery Answer.

Don't copy the behavior and customs of this world, but let God transform you into a new person by changing the way you think. Then you will learn to know God's will for you, which is good and pleasing and perfect.
ROMANS 12:2

ACROSS

1	EMANCIPATION	M E D E F O R
5	EXILE	G U R E F E E
6	SPOILS	S I N U R
7	OUTER LIMITS	D E E G S

DOWN

1	CULTIVATING	G R A F N I M
2	IMPOSE	F R E E C O N
3	UNEARTHING	G I G G N I D
4	COMES ACROSS	S E M E T

MYSTERY ANSWER:

CLUE: We do God's will by _____ to his plan.

GOD PROVIDES SALVATION

Complete the crossword puzzle by looking at the clues and unscrambling the answers. When the puzzle is complete, unscramble the circled letters to solve the Mystery Answer.

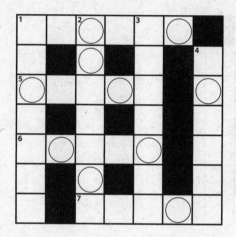

In [Christ] we have redemption through his blood, the forgiveness of sins, in accordance with the riches of God's grace.
EPHESIANS 1:7, NIV

ACROSS

1	REDUCED SPEED	WODLES
5	OBJECTS	ISMET
6	VALUE HIGHLY	ZIPER
7	ENTRIES	GESTA

DOWN

1	LOST FOOTING	PILPEDS
2	APERTURE	NENIPOG
3	LEAST DIFFICULT	ETASSIE
4	UPWARD FLIGHT	RASITS

MYSTERY ANSWER: ☐☐☐☐☐☐☐☐☐☐☐

CLUE: **The result of our purchase through Christ's blood.**

GOD IS A SAFE HAVEN

Complete the crossword puzzle by looking at the clues and unscrambling the answers. When the puzzle is complete, unscramble the circled letters to solve the Mystery Answer.

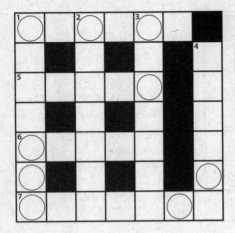

You have preserved my life because I am innocent; you have brought me into your presence forever.

PSALM 41:12

ACROSS

1	MISSISSIPPI AND HUDSON	**V I R R E S**
5	PHONES	**S L A C L**
6	IVORY KEYBOARD	**O N I P A**
7	HOLLERED	**T H U S E D O**

DOWN

1	FORMULAS	**E P I S C R E**
2	LAVA PRODUCER	**O V A L N O C**
3	FILM AGAIN	**T R E S O H O**
4	LED	**G U D D I E**

MYSTERY ANSWER:

CLUE: The Lord _____ his faithful followers.

24

GOD WELCOMES THE FAITHFUL INTO HIS FAMILY

Complete the crossword puzzle by looking at the clues and unscrambling the answers. When the puzzle is complete, unscramble the circled letters to solve the Mystery Answer.

You are no longer foreigners and aliens, but fellow citizens with God's people and members of God's household.

EPHESIANS 2:19, NIV

ACROSS

1	LADIES	MOWNE
4	MORE RECENT	WREEN
6	REGIONS	ERASA
7	ALL	VYREE

DOWN

1	TIMEPIECE	CHAWT
2	ARTIFICIAL	ENDMAMA
3	OBSCURE PLACE	WREENOH
5	TARNISHED	TURYS

MYSTERY ANSWER:

CLUE: Christ himself is the chief _____.

GOD KEEPS US SAFE

Complete the crossword puzzle by looking at the clues and unscrambling the answers. When the puzzle is complete, unscramble the circled letters to solve the Mystery Answer.

Fearing people is a dangerous trap, but trusting the LORD means safety.
PROVERBS 29:25

ACROSS

1 DOUGHNUT SHOP   **B E R K A Y**

4 CRATES   **A S C E S**

6 RECREATION   **E R S I L E U**

7 UNBENDING   **D I G R I**

DOWN

2 LOCKING LIPS   **I K S I G N S**

3 SAVED   **S C U D E E R**

4 HUE   **C R O O L**

5 BLOCKADE   **I G E E S**

MYSTERY ANSWER: ☐☐☐☐☐☐☐☐☐ ☐☐☐☐☐

CLUE: One who provides safety at busy intersections.

GOD EMPOWERS US

Complete the crossword puzzle by looking at the clues and unscrambling the answers. When the puzzle is complete, unscramble the circled letters to solve the Mystery Answer.

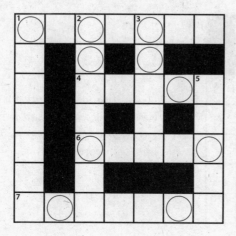

God has not given us a spirit of fear and timidity, but of power, love, and self-discipline.
2 TIMOTHY 1:7

ACROSS

1	WENT HUNGRY	V E D R A S T
4	INCREASED	D E D A D
6	MASSIVE DEER	E S O M O
7	CONCLUSIONS	S N I D G E N

DOWN

1	BIG SHOT	E N S E M O O
2	FRIGHTENED	L A M E D A R
3	CAPTURE ON TAPE	E D V O I
5	GOWN	S E R D S

MYSTERY ANSWER:

CLUE: Boldly sharing the good news with others.

GOD EXTENDS SACRIFICIAL LOVE

Complete the crossword puzzle by looking at the clues and unscrambling the answers. When the puzzle is complete, unscramble the circled letters to solve the Mystery Answer.

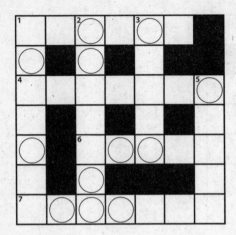

God loved the world so much that he gave his one and only Son, so that everyone who believes in him will not perish but have eternal life.

JOHN 3:16

ACROSS

1	OF THE TEETH	E N D L A T
4	TAPERS	W A R N R O S
6	COMMAND	O R R E D
7	METHODS	S E M S T Y S

DOWN

1	BALLERINAS	C R A N S E D
2	JITTERY	E N R O V U S
3	AUDIBLY	U L A D O
5	CLASSIFIES	T R O S S

MYSTERY ANSWER:

⬜⬜⬜⬜⬜⬜ ⬜⬜⬜⬜⬜⬜

CLUE: **When we celebrate Christ's triumph over death.**

28

GOD BLESSES BELIEVERS

Complete the crossword puzzle by looking at the clues and unscrambling the answers. When the puzzle is complete, unscramble the circled letters to solve the Mystery Answer.

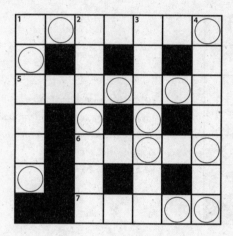

There is no difference between Jew and Gentile—the same Lord is Lord of all and richly blesses all who call on him.

ROMANS 10:12, NIV

ACROSS

1 RESPONSES   SEEPRIL

5 EXHIBITION   WISHNOG

6 REFLECTION   AIMEG

7 OCCASION   TEVNE

DOWN

1 VACATION SPOT   TREORS

2 COVENANT   PREMOSI

3 COPY   TAITIME

4 PORTION   NEGMEST

MYSTERY ANSWER: ⬜⬜⬜   ⬜⬜⬜⬜⬜⬜⬜⬜⬜⬜

CLUE: Record of Jesus' ministry and the early church.

GOD SAVES HIS OWN

Complete the crossword puzzle by looking at the clues and unscrambling the answers. When the puzzle is complete, unscramble the circled letters to solve the Mystery Answer.

[Jesus] is able, once and forever, to save those who come to God through him. He lives forever to intercede with God on their behalf.

HEBREWS 7:25

ACROSS

1	MOST DESIRABLE	DIALE
4	POWDERY	UDYTS
6	SWEET BIRTHDAY	EXINEST
7	ESPIES	GISSTH

DOWN

1	CATALOG	NEXDI
2	PRODUCING EGGS	AYLNIG
3	HESITATES	SUPASE
5	CLEANED THE FLOOR	PEWTS

MYSTERY ANSWER: ☐☐☐☐ ☐ ☐☐☐☐

CLUE: Offer assistance.

GOD DESTROYS THE PROUD

Complete the crossword puzzle by looking at the clues and unscrambling the answers. When the puzzle is complete, unscramble the circled letters to solve the Mystery Answer.

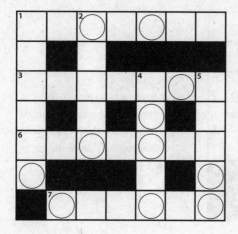

The LORD tears down the house of the proud, but he protects the property of widows.
PROVERBS 15:25

ACROSS

1	BEACH MALADY	RUNNUBS
3	ORGANIZE	RARANEG
6	USING MOLARS	WECNIGH
7	NIGHTFALL	SESTUN

DOWN

1	SHIRT STIFFENER	RATSCH
2	GUTS	REVEN
4	PERFORMS PERFECTLY	SILAN
5	SKATER'S FIGURE	IGETH

MYSTERY ANSWER:

CLUE: God destroys this in the proud.

31

GOD PROTECTS US FROM DISASTER

Complete the crossword puzzle by looking at the clues and unscrambling the answers. When the puzzle is complete, unscramble the circled letters to solve the Mystery Answer.

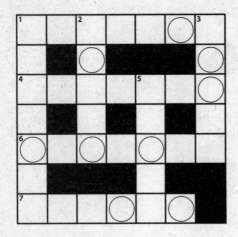

Have mercy on me, O God, have mercy! I look to you for protection. I will hide beneath the shadow of your wings until the danger passes by.
PSALM 57:1

ACROSS

1	GAVE A PRIZE	DAREWAD
4	SEA CREATURE	PUSTOCO
6	PRAIRIE TWISTER	OTODRAN
7	PASTRY	ASHIND

DOWN

1	TOOK ON	PEDDOAT
2	THESPIAN	CORTA
3	SEVENTIES NIGHTCLUB	CIDOS
5	SUMMITS	ASKEP

MYSTERY ANSWER: ☐☐☐☐☐☐☐☐☐☐☐

CLUE: Relief organizations.

GOD EXTENDS FREEDOM

Complete the crossword puzzle by looking at the clues and unscrambling the answers. When the puzzle is complete, unscramble the circled letters to solve the Mystery Answer.

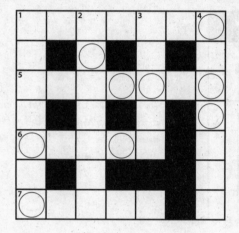

Evil people will surely be punished, but the children of the godly will go free.

PROVERBS 11:21

ACROSS

1	CONGRATULATE	PALUDAP
5	TRIUMPH	COVIRTY
6	ELEVATE	ASERI
7	EXCITED	AGREE

DOWN

1	CONTRARY	SEREVAD
2	CHIPPING AWAY AT	KEPCING
3	STOPPED SLEEPING	OWAEK
4	SHIP REPAIR SITE	RODDYCK

MYSTERY ANSWER:

CLUE: God promises that evil will be _____.

33

GOD PROTECTS US WITH ANGELS

Complete the crossword puzzle by looking at the clues and unscrambling the answers. When the puzzle is complete, unscramble the circled letters to solve the Mystery Answer.

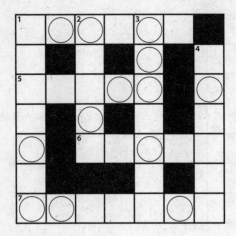

The angel of the LORD encamps around those who fear him, and he delivers them.

PSALM 34:7, NIV

ACROSS

1	CONNECT	G A N E E G
5	MORE ANCIENT	L O E R D
6	GAUGE OF AGE	A R S E Y
7	ATOMIC	A L R U C E N

DOWN

1	WEAR AND TEAR	S E O R I O N
2	LIGHTHEADED	D I G Y D
3	TRASH	B E G G A R A
4	MORE INTIMATE	L O R E S C

MYSTERY ANSWER:

CLUE: One whom the Lord sends for protection.

GOD IS ALWAYS PRESENT

Complete the crossword puzzle by looking at the clues and unscrambling the answers. When the puzzle is complete, unscramble the circled letters to solve the Mystery Answer.

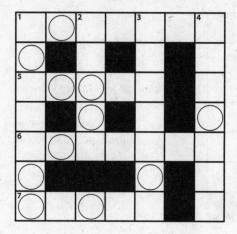

God is our refuge and strength, always ready to help in times of trouble.
PSALM 46:1

ACROSS

1	EATING	ZIGGARN
5	SORROW	GREFI
6	FOLKLORE	SEDLENG
7	BAGS	CASSK

DOWN

1	SAFETY GLASSES	GESGLOG
2	GETTING OLDER	GANGI
3	NEWBORNS	FATNNIS
4	STABS IN THE DARK	SESESUG

MYSTERY ANSWER:

CLUE: One who prays on our behalf.

GOD LEADS HIS PEOPLE TO THEIR PROMISED LAND

Complete the crossword puzzle by looking at the clues and unscrambling the answers. When the puzzle is complete, unscramble the circled letters to solve the Mystery Answer.

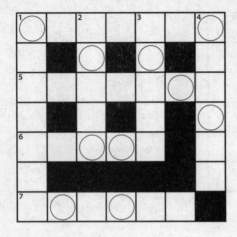

I am with you, and I will protect you wherever you go. One day I will bring you back to this land. I will not leave you until I have finished giving you everything I have promised you.
GENESIS 28:15

ACROSS

1	DISTANT	W A F R A Y A
5	ONSET	R A L A V I R
6	STOPS	A L S H T
7	SUSPICIOUS	F I S Y T H

DOWN

1	FLICKERS	L A S H E F S
2	RUSTIC	L U R R A
3	SPOUSES	V I S W E
4	GOLDEN HUE	L E Y W O L

MYSTERY ANSWER:

CLUE: How God shepherds his people.

GOD PROVIDES FIRM FOUNDATIONS

Complete the crossword puzzle by looking at the clues and unscrambling the answers. When the puzzle is complete, unscramble the circled letters to solve the Mystery Answer.

Unless the LORD builds a house, the work of the builders is wasted.... It is useless for you to work so hard from early morning until late at night, anxiously working for food to eat; for God gives rest to his loved ones.
PSALM 127:1-2

ACROSS

1	WEASELS	BASSEL
3	PERFORMANCE	CLARETI
6	CANARY AND CAYMAN	LINDSAS
7	QUOTES	TISCE

DOWN

1	RAIDS	OSETIRS
2	VANISHED	CINTEXT
4	TUMMY ACHE	LOCCI
5	MISPLACES	SOLSE

MYSTERY ANSWER:

CLUE: Material used to build a foundation.

GOD CROWNS OUR EFFORTS

Complete the crossword puzzle by looking at the clues and unscrambling the answers. When the puzzle is complete, unscramble the circled letters to solve the Mystery Answer.

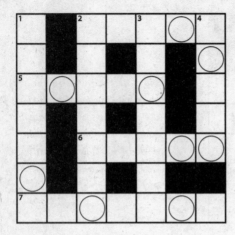

God blesses those who patiently endure testing and temptation. Afterward they will receive the crown of life that God has promised to those who love him. And remember, when you are being tempted, do not say, "God is tempting me." God is never tempted to do wrong, and he never tempts anyone else.

JAMES 1:12-13

ACROSS

2	SMALL FLUTES	SEFFI
5	PIONEER CARRIAGE	WONGA
6	PLAY AGAIN	NURRE
7	READIED A HORSE	DADSLED

DOWN

1	PROSECUTORS	SWALERY
2	SUPPOSED	UGIRDEF
3	MEMORIAL SERVICE	LUNFREA
4	DISDAIN	RONCS

MYSTERY ANSWER:

CLUE: **Ability to withstand hardship.**

38

GOD DELIVERS FROM SIN

Complete the crossword puzzle by looking at the clues and unscrambling the answers. When the puzzle is complete, unscramble the circled letters to solve the Mystery Answer.

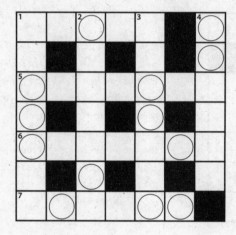

Humble yourselves before God. Resist the devil, and he will flee from you.
JAMES 4:7

ACROSS

1 FUNNY   C O C I M

5 DRAW   C A T T A R T

6 FAREWELL   O D Y B E G O

7 WANT DESPERATELY   R E E S I D

DOWN

1 TRANSITIONED   D E N C A G H

2 WAYS   S H M E D O T

3 COMPARTMENT   R A B M E C H

4 FROTH   A R T H E L

MYSTERY ANSWER:

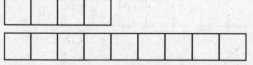

CLUE: A woman whom Jesus delivered from a life of sin.

39

GOD BLESSES REVERENCE

Complete the crossword puzzle by looking at the clues and unscrambling the answers. When the puzzle is complete, unscramble the circled letters to solve the Mystery Answer.

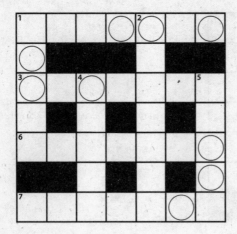

How joyful are those who fear the LORD—all who follow his ways! You will enjoy the fruit of your labor. How joyful and prosperous you will be! Your wife will be like a fruitful grapevine, flourishing within your home. Your children will be like vigorous young olive trees as they sit around your table. That is the LORD's blessing for those who fear him.

PSALM 128:1-4

ACROSS

1	FIXES	**P R A I S E R**
3	FIRST TO FINISH	**T E S S F A T**
6	CONVEY	**X E S P E R S**
7	REPAIR SHOPS	**S A G G A R E**

DOWN

1	FIREARM	**F E R L I**
2	CRISPY LETTUCE	**E B E C R I G**
4	FANTASTIC	**P U R E S**
5	TRIES	**S E T T S**

MYSTERY ANSWER:

CLUE: The Lord _____ all who fear him.

40

GOD IS ACCESSIBLE

Complete the crossword puzzle by looking at the clues and unscrambling the answers. When the puzzle is complete, unscramble the circled letters to solve the Mystery Answer.

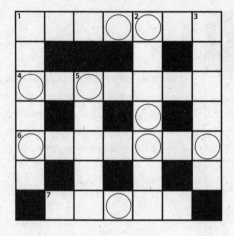

[Jesus] came and preached peace to you who were far away and peace to those who were near. For through him we both have access to the Father by one Spirit.

EPHESIANS 2:17-18, NIV

ACROSS

1	COUNSELED	DADSEVI
4	TEETER-TOTTERS	WASESES
6	MORE JOLLY	REEMIRR
7	LEGENDS	STYHM

DOWN

1	SUPPOSE	SUMSEA
2	ROMANCE LANGUAGE	HIPNASS
3	WASTELAND	DRETES
5	PREMATURE	LYREA

MYSTERY ANSWER: ⬚⬚⬚⬚⬚⬚⬚⬚⬚⬚⬚⬚

CLUE: **People who bring spiritual encouragement.**

GOD GIVES GRACE

Complete the crossword puzzle by looking at the clues and unscrambling the answers. When the puzzle is complete, unscramble the circled letters to solve the Mystery Answer.

God saved you by his grace when you believed. And you can't take credit for this; it is a gift from God. Salvation is not a reward for the good things we have done, so none of us can boast about it.

EPHESIANS 2:8-9

ACROSS

1	GRANNY SMITH	**P E L P A**
4	STUMBLED	**P E R P D I T**
6	TROPICAL FRUIT	**N O O C C U T**
7	EXPERTS	**M E R S S A T**

DOWN

1	TOP STORY	**T A C I T**
2	ROYAL SONS	**S P E R C I N**
3	COST	**X E S N E E P**
5	PALM TREE SWEETS	**S A T E D**

MYSTERY ANSWER:

CLUE: **A branch of the Christian church, launched in A.D. 1517.**

GOD ENCOURAGES US

Complete the crossword puzzle by looking at the clues and unscrambling the answers. When the puzzle is complete, unscramble the circled letters to solve the Mystery Answer.

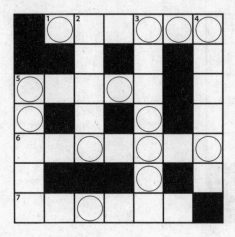

Now may our Lord Jesus Christ himself and God our Father, who loved us and by his grace gave us eternal comfort and a wonderful hope, comfort you and strengthen you in every good thing you do and say.

2 THESSALONIANS 2:16-17

ACROSS

1 OBJECTS   **N I G H T S**

5 METAL FASTENER   **W E R S C**

6 OLYMPIAN   **T H E A T E L**

7 LEASED   **D R E E N T**

DOWN

2 SEVERE   **S H H R A**

3 NOT TO BE FOUND   **H E E W O R N**

4 STOCKHOLM LOCATION   **N S E E D W**

5 SINGLE STEP   **T A S I R**

MYSTERY ANSWER:

CLUE: God's promise of encouragement.

43

GOD BLESSES DUTIFUL CHILDREN

Complete the crossword puzzle by looking at the clues and unscrambling the answers. When the puzzle is complete, unscramble the circled letters to solve the Mystery Answer.

Direct your children onto the right path, and when they are older, they will not leave it.
PROVERBS 22:6

ACROSS

1	ARTIST'S WORKSHOP	**U S I D O T**
5	TITHE	**N E T H T**
6	MOTORLESS BOAT	**N O C E A**
7	ROBIN HOMES	**T E N S S**

DOWN

2	HAZARDS	**D R E S A N G**
3	ADDITIONAL	**T H R O E**
4	SMOKED SWINE	**O B A N C**
5	MELODIES	**N U E S T**

MYSTERY ANSWER:

CLUE: **Children need this to honor their parents.**

GOD OFFERS HOPE

Complete the crossword puzzle by looking at the clues and unscrambling the answers. When the puzzle is complete, unscramble the circled letters to solve the Mystery Answer.

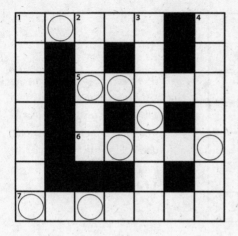

Our present troubles are small and won't last very long. Yet they produce for us a glory that vastly outweighs them and will last forever!

2 CORINTHIANS 4:17

ACROSS

1	MORAL PRINCIPLE	H I C E T
5	COMPANY OF LIONS	D I R P E
6	LARIATS	O S E R P
7	PRONOUNCED	O N U S E D D

DOWN

1	HARD WORK	F R E T S O F
2	HIGH-STRUNG	P H E R Y
3	FASTENED	P E C P I L D
4	CONTENT	D A L E E P S

MYSTERY ANSWER:

CLUE: Like a strong pillar, God _____ us during troubled times.

GOD MAKES US HIS CHILDREN

Complete the crossword puzzle by looking at the clues and unscrambling the answers. When the puzzle is complete, unscramble the circled letters to solve the Mystery Answer.

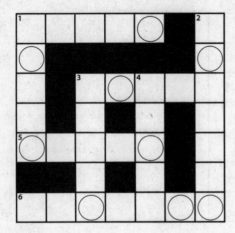

How great is the love the Father has lavished on us, that we should be called children of God! And that is what we are! The reason the world does not know us is that it did not know him.

1 JOHN 3:1, NIV

ACROSS

1	SPRING CHICKEN	**G U N O Y**
3	DAD'S SISTERS	**A S T U N**
5	GIVE SHELTER TO	**S H U O E**
6	CARES FOR	**S H O R T M E**

DOWN

1	ADOLESCENCE	**U H O Y T**
2	GROUP OF NUNS	**T I S S E R S**
3	GROWN-UP	**U D T A L**
4	BROTHER'S DAUGHTER	**I C E E N**

MYSTERY ANSWER:

CLUE: God wants his children to be _____.

46

GOD WILL UNITE US WITH CHRIST

Complete the crossword puzzle by looking at the clues and unscrambling the answers. When the puzzle is complete, unscramble the circled letters to solve the Mystery Answer.

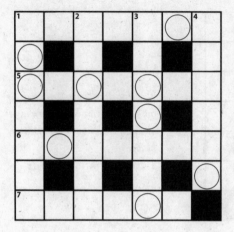

We tell you this directly from the Lord: We who are still living when the Lord returns will not meet him ahead of those who have died. For the Lord himself will come down from heaven with a commanding shout, with the voice of the archangel, and with the trumpet call of God. First, the Christians who have died will rise from their graves. Then, together with them, we who are still alive and remain on the earth will be caught up in the clouds to meet the Lord in the air. Then we will be with the Lord forever. So encourage each other with these words.
1 THESSALONIANS 4:15-18

ACROSS

1 STROLLERS   **B L A M E R S**

5 SEASIDE   **A C A L O S T**

6 MISERY   **S E D S A N S**

7 DARTED   **G O D D E D**

DOWN

1 BLAMED   **C A S C U D E**

2 EMBARKED   **B R O D D E A**

3 ULTIMATE   **E R X M E T E**

4 SPATTER   **S H A L P S**

MYSTERY ANSWER: ⬜⬜⬜⬜⬜⬜⬜⬜⬜⬜⬜

CLUE: Christ's followers should imitate his _____.

47

GOD WILL RESTORE US

Complete the crossword puzzle by looking at the clues and unscrambling the answers. When the puzzle is complete, unscramble the circled letters to solve the Mystery Answer.

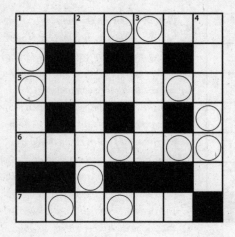

We do not lose heart. Though outwardly we are wasting away, yet inwardly we are being renewed day by day.

2 CORINTHIANS 4:16, NIV

ACROSS

1	MOST ACTIVE	**USBESTI**
5	HAMMERING	**INNAGLI**
6	PROVIDE COVER	**SLEERTH**
7	RETORT	**WRENAS**

DOWN

1	DEPOSITS	**KNABS**
2	CREEPY-CRAWLIES	**DRIPESS**
3	LIVE	**XISET**
4	STRIPED CATS	**GRIEST**

MYSTERY ANSWER: ☐☐☐☐☐ ☐☐☐☐☐☐☐☐

CLUE: Despite our outward circumstances, God provides this every day.

GOD PREPARES US A HEAVENLY HOME

Complete the crossword puzzle by looking at the clues and unscrambling the answers. When the puzzle is complete, unscramble the circled letters to solve the Mystery Answer.

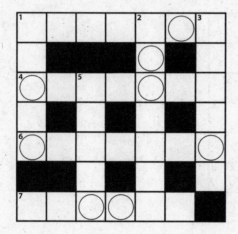

We know that when this earthly tent we live in is taken down (that is, when we die and leave this earthly body), we will have a house in heaven, an eternal body made for us by God himself and not by human hands.
2 CORINTHIANS 5:1

ACROSS

1 MORE GOOFY   L I R S I L E

4 BOLTING   C O N K L I G

6 GRASP   L A R E Z I E

7 ORBIT   C R I C E L

DOWN

1 SUN POWER   L O R A S

2 FIRST   T I N I A L I

3 RUE   G E R T E R

5 COMMITTEE HEAD   H I R C A

MYSTERY ANSWER:

CLUE: Family-room fixture.

GOD CREATES ENJOYMENT

Complete the crossword puzzle by looking at the clues and unscrambling the answers. When the puzzle is complete, unscramble the circled letters to solve the Mystery Answer.

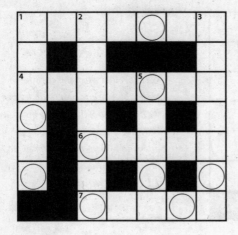

Their trust should be in God, who richly gives us all we need for our enjoyment.
1 TIMOTHY 6:17

ACROSS

1	COLORFUL PROMISE	B O A R W I N
4	VEGGIE DRAWER	C E R R P S I
6	PERCH	D E E L G
7	WORM FIBERS	S K I L S

DOWN

1	BRING TO MIND	L R E C L A
2	FROZEN DRIPS	C I L S E I C
3	SOME BEES	R E S K R O W
5	TREADLE	P L E A D

MYSTERY ANSWER: ☐☐☐☐☐☐☐☐☐☐☐

CLUE: Fenway and Wrigley.

50

GOD OFFERS A CLEAN SLATE

Complete the crossword puzzle by looking at the clues and unscrambling the answers. When the puzzle is complete, unscramble the circled letters to solve the Mystery Answer.

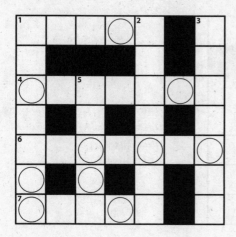

Repent of your sins and turn to God, so that your sins may be wiped away. Then times of refreshment will come from the presence of the Lord.
ACTS 3:19-20

ACROSS

1 BLANCHES   L E P S A

4 ANALYZE   P O X E L E R

6 JUSTIFY   P A L I N E X

7 OLYMPIC FIRE   C O R T H

DOWN

1 HERE AND NOW   R E T P E N S

2 TOLERATE   S H A C M O T

3 LAUNDERED   N E C A L D E

5 ESSAY   P R E P A

MYSTERY ANSWER: ⬚⬚⬚⬚⬚⬚⬚⬚⬚⬚⬚

CLUE: Necessary for the forgiveness of sins.

GOD LISTENS TO YOUR NEEDS

Complete the crossword puzzle by looking at the clues and unscrambling the answers. When the puzzle is complete, unscramble the circled letters to solve the Mystery Answer.

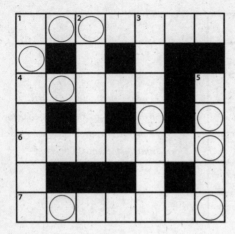

Listen! The Lord's arm is not too weak to save you, nor is his ear too deaf to hear you call.

ISAIAH 59:1

ACROSS

1 BOUNDARY   **S M A C O P S**

4 CHECKS   **S E N I R**

6 LEAST DIFFICULT   **T I E S E S A**

7 PANT   **R O R U T E S**

DOWN

1 ACCURATE   **T R E C O R C**

2 HOUSEKEEPERS   **M A S I D**

3 PAINFUL SORE   **S C A B E S S**

5 SUBSEQUENT   **R E F T A**

MYSTERY ANSWER:

CLUE: **One who gives strength and hope.**

GOD HOLDS PEOPLE ACCOUNTABLE

Complete the crossword puzzle by looking at the clues and unscrambling the answers. When the puzzle is complete, unscramble the circled letters to solve the Mystery Answer.

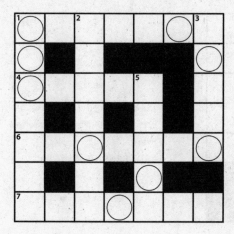

Yes, each of us will give a personal account to God.
ROMANS 14:12

ACROSS

1	NOVELS	C O N T I F I
4	NOT SMALL	G R A L E
6	ISLAND OF CORK	L I N A E R D
7	COLLECTS	T H E G R A S

DOWN

1	MAKING COMPACT	D I G F L O N
2	PRESENT	E R R T U N C
3	CALLED	M A N D E
5	WIPE OUT	A R S E E

MYSTERY ANSWER:

CLUE: Absence of truth.

53

GOD GIVES RICH BLESSINGS

Complete the crossword puzzle by looking at the clues and unscrambling the answers. When the puzzle is complete, unscramble the circled letters to solve the Mystery Answer.

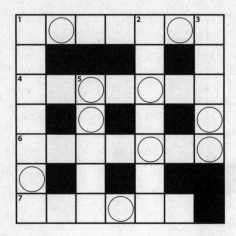

*The blessing of the L*ORD *makes a person rich, and he adds no sorrow with it.*
PROVERBS 10:22

ACROSS

1	BURIES	**N E M B O S T**
4	KNOCK FLAT	**N E A P A C K**
6	TEN DECADES	**E N T R U C Y**
7	FASHIONS	**S L E S T Y**

DOWN

1	ANTICIPATES	**C S E P T E X**
2	AMOUNT	**S E A M E R U**
3	RUN-DOWN	**D Y E S E**
5	CHILD'S CAREGIVER	**N Y N A N**

MYSTERY ANSWER:

CLUE: **How God chooses to bless those who love him.**

54

GOD PROTECTS HIS OWN

Complete the crossword puzzle by looking at the clues and unscrambling the answers. When the puzzle is complete, unscramble the circled letters to solve the Mystery Answer.

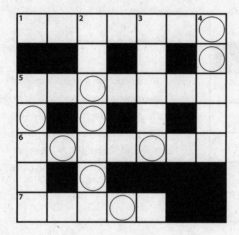

Though I am surrounded by troubles, you will protect me from the anger of my enemies. You reach out your hand, and the power of your right hand saves me.

PSALM 138:7

ACROSS

1	SEEDED	T A L N P E D
5	STUDY OF MATTER AND ENERGY	S P I S C H Y
6	INCORRECTLY	W Y N L O R G
7	IMPERIAL	L O R A Y

DOWN

2	SOMEONE	D O N B Y A Y
3	OBJECT	N I G H T
4	SHADOWY	S K U D Y
5	MIGHT	P R E W O

MYSTERY ANSWER:

CLUE: **Powerful protector.**

GOD WILL APPEAR TO ALL

Complete the crossword puzzle by looking at the clues and unscrambling the answers. When the puzzle is complete, unscramble the circled letters to solve the Mystery Answer.

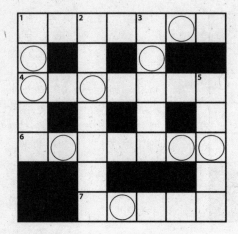

Think about the things of heaven, not the things of earth. For you died to this life, and your real life is hidden with Christ in God. And when Christ, who is your life, is revealed to the whole world, you will share in all his glory.

COLOSSIANS 3:2-4

ACROSS

1	SNATCHED	**BEDBRAG**
4	PUTS ON	**PELSAPI**
6	PULLED	**GRADGED**
7	WANDER	**TASRY**

DOWN

1	KEEP SAFE	**RUDAG**
2	BECOMES VISIBLE	**EPASPAR**
3	CONVEY	**GRINB**
5	SOAPY	**DUSSY**

MYSTERY ANSWER:

CLUE: **Leaving this world behind.**

GOD DIRECTS HIS PEOPLE

Complete the crossword puzzle by looking at the clues and unscrambling the answers. When the puzzle is complete, unscramble the circled letters to solve the Mystery Answer.

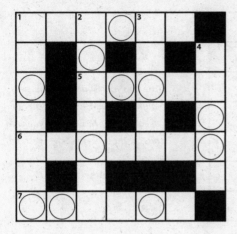

The commandments of the LORD are right, bringing joy to the heart. The commands of the LORD are clear, giving insight for living.

PSALM 19:8

ACROSS

1	PLETHORA	L A T W E H
5	IN THE COUNTRY	R A L R U
6	CORRIDOR	H A W A L L Y
7	WASTEWATER	G E E S A W

DOWN

1	BURDENS	W I G S T E H
2	CROSS BREEZE	F L A I R O W
3	TOSSED	W R E T H
4	RUSES	P L Y S O

MYSTERY ANSWER:

CLUE: How should we follow God's commands?

GOD DELIGHTS IN HIS CHILDREN

Complete the crossword puzzle by looking at the clues and unscrambling the answers. When the puzzle is complete, unscramble the circled letters to solve the Mystery Answer.

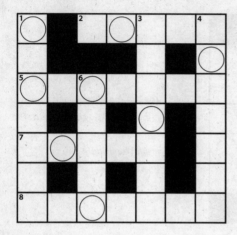

The LORD your God is with you, he is mighty to save. He will take great delight in you, he will quiet you with his love, he will rejoice over you with singing.
ZEPHANIAH 3:17, NIV

ACROSS

2	WAKE-UP CALL	L A M A R
5	CONFIDENT	D R E S U A S
7	GREETING	L O L E H
8	MORE SUGARY	E R S T E W E

DOWN

1	EXTENDS	A C R E E S H
3	LANDING FIELD	R I T O A R P
4	MURKIER	D U M E R D I
6	DECIPHER	E L V S O

MYSTERY ANSWER:

CLUE: God's creation gives him _____.

GOD GIVES US A PLACE TO BELONG

Complete the crossword puzzle by looking at the clues and unscrambling the answers. When the puzzle is complete, unscramble the circled letters to solve the Mystery Answer.

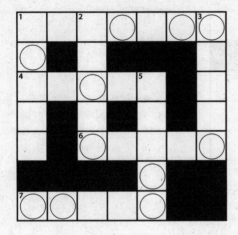

The LORD will not abandon his people, because that would dishonor his great name. For it has pleased the LORD to make you his very own people.

1 SAMUEL 12:22

ACROSS

1	SLAPPING LIGHTLY	P I N G A T T
4	DIRECTORY	N I X E D
6	AGES	S E A R Y
7	DISTRIBUTES	D O S L E

DOWN

1	ARTIST'S MEDIUM	P I N A T
2	PRESENT	D O A T Y
3	EXPANDS	W R O G S
5	DIAGNOSTIC TESTS	S A X Y R

MYSTERY ANSWER: ☐☐☐☐ ' ☐☐ ☐☐☐☐☐☐☐☐☐

CLUE: **Exclusive membership for Christ's heirs.**

GOD EMPOWERS LEADERS

Complete the crossword puzzle by looking at the clues and unscrambling the answers. When the puzzle is complete, unscramble the circled letters to solve the Mystery Answer.

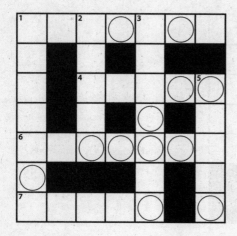

This is my command—be strong and courageous! Do not be afraid or discouraged. For the LORD your God is with you wherever you go.

JOSHUA 1:9

ACROSS

1	WEAR OUT	THAXUSE
4	PARCHED	DEKBA
6	RESULT	MOCOTEU
7	INGESTED	ETNEA

DOWN

1	IDEAL EXAMPLE	IMOTEEP
2	REPETITIVE ACTION	BATHI
3	ANONYMOUS	WONKUNN
5	SLUMBER VISION	ERMDA

MYSTERY ANSWER:

CLUE: Ten to obey.

GOD CARES FOR THE HUMBLE

Complete the crossword puzzle by looking at the clues and unscrambling the answers. When the puzzle is complete, unscramble the circled letters to solve the Mystery Answer.

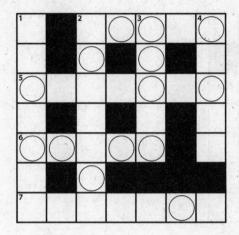

Though the LORD is great, he cares for the humble, but he keeps his distance from the proud.
PSALM 138:6

ACROSS

2 WHISKER ELIMINATOR   A R R O Z

5 HINDER   B L A S I D E

6 PORCELAIN   A C H N I

7 ICE AGAIN   G R A Z E L E

DOWN

1 BIKER ACCESSORY   A C R I D E S

2 HURRYING   H U N S I R G

3 STRIPED MAMMAL   R E Z A B

4 TALL GRASSES   S E D E R

MYSTERY ANSWER:

CLUE: **Old Testament king whom God humbled and restored.**

GOD FORGETS OUR SINS

Complete the crossword puzzle by looking at the clues and unscrambling the answers. When the puzzle is complete, unscramble the circled letters to solve the Mystery Answer.

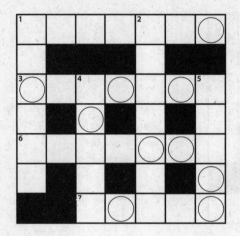

I—yes, I alone—will blot out your sins for my own sake and will never think of them again.

ISAIAH 43:25

ACROSS

1	UNSMILING	PADDENA
3	PREFERRED	VEFRADO
6	LACK	CABENES
7	SWEET BLOOMS	ORESS

DOWN

1	BEAT	FEEDAT
2	BRINGS FORTH	SARPTEN
4	SUNSHADE	SOVIR
5	CLOTHE	SERDS

MYSTERY ANSWER:

CLUE: Admitting sins and seeking forgiveness.

GOD PROVIDES ETERNAL RICHES

Complete the crossword puzzle by looking at the clues and unscrambling the answers. When the puzzle is complete, unscramble the circled letters to solve the Mystery Answer.

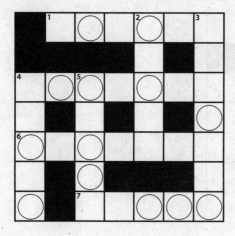

Where your treasure is, there your heart will be also.

LUKE 12:34, NIV

ACROSS

1 SOVIET REPUBLIC — A R S I U S

4 FEMALE PRONOUN — E L S F E R H

6 CITY CONGESTION — I F T C A R F

7 PASTRIES — S R A T T

DOWN

2 MANTELPIECE — F L E S H

3 INFLUENCES — S E F T C A F

4 RABBIT CAGE — T H U C H

5 OPPOSE A FORCE — C E T R A

MYSTERY ANSWER:

CLUE: **Collection of valuables.**

63

GOD IS OUR CONSTANT COMPANION

Complete the crossword puzzle by looking at the clues and unscrambling the answers. When the puzzle is complete, unscramble the circled letters to solve the Mystery Answer.

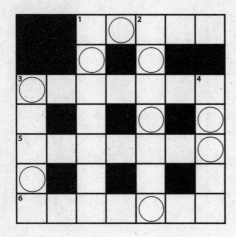

God has said, "Never will I leave you; never will I forsake you."
HEBREWS 13:5, NIV

ACROSS

1 SQUANDER   **S W E A T**

3 LACK OF SUCCESS   **R I E F U L A**

5 AUTHORS   **S I R R W E T**

6 CORRECTLY   **H Y R G I L T**

DOWN

1 PASSING TIME   **I T W I G A N**

2 PUPIL   **D U N S E T T**

3 LESS   **E F R E W**

4 COMPOSITION   **S A Y S E**

MYSTERY ANSWER: ☐☐☐☐☐☐☐☐☐

CLUE: We can rest in God's _____ presence.

GOD HELPS US OVERCOME OUR FEARS

Complete the crossword puzzle by looking at the clues and unscrambling the answers. When the puzzle is complete, unscramble the circled letters to solve the Mystery Answer.

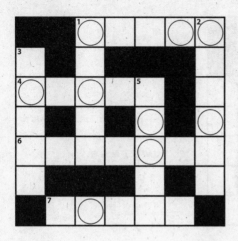

I hold you by your right hand—I, the LORD your God. And I say to you, "Don't be afraid. I am here to help you."

ISAIAH 41:13

ACROSS

1	FREIGHT	ROGCA
4	OPT FOR	CLEET
6	POD	PELUSCA
7	COLLAPSED	VADEC

DOWN

1	CUT-RATE	HAPEC
2	UNSEALED	PENDOE
3	CLEMENCY	CYREM
5	ARMISTICE	ERUCT

MYSTERY ANSWER: ⬚⬚⬚⬚⬚⬚⬚⬚⬚⬚

CLUE: Offer a hand.

GOD DESIRES TO BE CLOSE TO YOU

Complete the crossword puzzle by looking at the clues and unscrambling the answers. When the puzzle is complete, unscramble the circled letters to solve the Mystery Answer.

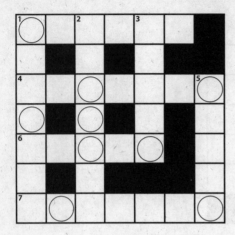

Come near to God and he will come near to you.

JAMES 4:8, NIV

ACROSS

1	PRODS	W E L S O B
4	DEER ENEMIES	U N R E S H T
6	STRAPS	B L E S T
7	LETTING FLY	S T O G S I N

DOWN

1	DISPLAY	I B E X I T H
2	BOUND PACKAGES	N U D S B L E
3	SEVEN-DAY CYCLES	K W E S E
5	TRY TO HOMER	G W I S N

MYSTERY ANSWER:

CLUE: Cleanliness is said to be next to this.

GOD LOVES INFINITELY THROUGH CHRIST

Complete the crossword puzzle by looking at the clues and unscrambling the answers. When the puzzle is complete, unscramble the circled letters to solve the Mystery Answer.

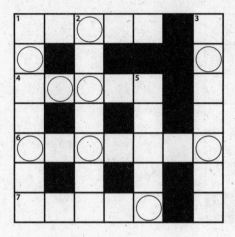

I pray that you, being rooted and established in love, may have power, together with all the saints, to grasp how wide and long and high and deep is the love of Christ, and to know this love that surpasses knowledge—that you may be filled to the measure of all the fullness of God.

EPHESIANS 3:17-19, NIV

ACROSS

1 LOWER BODY JOINTS   E N S K E

4 EXPRESS GRATITUDE   H A T K N

6 REQUIRES   P E X C E S T

7 MOLTS   D E S S H

DOWN

1 FUZZY FELINES   N E T S I K T

2 DEMONSTRATION   E P A X M E L

3 DEVOTES   V E N T S I S

5 THRILLS   C I S K K

MYSTERY ANSWER:

CLUE: New Testament letter.

67

GOD GIVES EVERLASTING LIFE

Complete the crossword puzzle by looking at the clues and unscrambling the answers. When the puzzle is complete, unscramble the circled letters to solve the Mystery Answer.

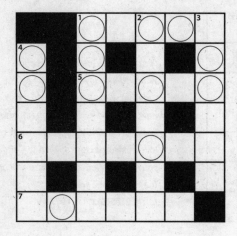

Jesus told her, "I am the resurrection and the life. Anyone who believes in me will live, even after dying. Everyone who lives in me and believes in me will never ever die."
JOHN 11:25-26

ACROSS

1	DARNED	E D E W S
5	FINGERTIPS	L A S N I
6	TYRANT	N O R T S E M
7	INSIST	M A D D E N

DOWN

1	SAME MEANING	M Y S O N N Y
2	PRINTED	E N T W I R T
3	WISH FOR	E D R E S I
4	GAVE THE IMPRESSION	E D S E M E

MYSTERY ANSWER:

CLUE: The disciples were _____ to Jesus' ministry.

GOD GRANTS SUCCESS

Complete the crossword puzzle by looking at the clues and unscrambling the answers. When the puzzle is complete, unscramble the circled letters to solve the Mystery Answer.

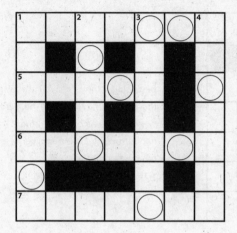

Commit your actions to the LORD, and your plans will succeed.

PROVERBS 16:3

ACROSS

1	SHOW FAVOR	PROVAPE
5	MEDIATOR	ANTGE
6	LACK HOPE	DISAERP
7	FIRM	DIDCEED

DOWN

1	PRESENTED A TROPHY	REWDADA
2	LYRICAL COMPOSERS	ETSPO
3	EXTERNAL	RODAWUT
4	WENT INTO	TRENDEE

MYSTERY ANSWER:

CLUE: Daily exercise that helps to focus your mind and spirit.

GOD OFFERS PEACE

Complete the crossword puzzle by looking at the clues and unscrambling the answers. When the puzzle is complete, unscramble the circled letters to solve the Mystery Answer.

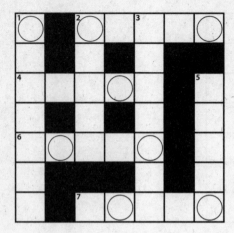

[Jesus said,] "I have told you all this so that you may have peace in me. Here on earth you will have many trials and sorrows. But take heart, because I have overcome the world."

JOHN 16:33

ACROSS

2	ONE OF DAVID'S WRITINGS	**S L A M P**
4	PLACE OF WORSHIP	**T R A L A**
6	PENTATEUCH	**R O A T H**
7	PETER'S NAME	**M I N S O**

DOWN

1	BOOK DIVISION	**H A R P E C T**
2	GIVE OUT	**E T R E P**
3	PATRIARCHS' PATRIARCH	**B A H M A A R**
5	HUMAN TEMPTER	**A N A T S**

MYSTERY ANSWER:

CLUE: Christ is our _____ in times of trouble.

GOD PROVIDES FAMILIES

Complete the crossword puzzle by looking at the clues and unscrambling the answers. When the puzzle is complete, unscramble the circled letters to solve the Mystery Answer.

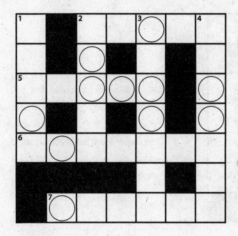

God places the lonely in families.
PSALM 68:6

ACROSS

2	DIRECT ELSEWHERE	R E F R E
5	JOCKEY	I R R D E
6	RESULT	P O D C R U T
7	REFINEMENT	I C E Y N T

DOWN

1	LEFTOVER	C A R P S
2	AIRWAVES	A R O D I
3	WEALTH	T R E N O U F
4	IN A CORRECT MANNER	G L Y T I R H

MYSTERY ANSWER: ☐☐☐☐☐☐☐☐☐☐☐☐

CLUE: Family patriarch.

71

GOD PROLONGS LIFE

Complete the crossword puzzle by looking at the clues and unscrambling the answers. When the puzzle is complete, unscramble the circled letters to solve the Mystery Answer.

My child, never forget the things I have taught you. Store my commands in your heart. If you do this, you will live many years, and your life will be satisfying.

PROVERBS 3:1-2

ACROSS

1	PEARLY WHITES	**H E T T E**
4	HONKER	**E S O G O**
5	VISITOR	**E U G S T**
6	PROPERTY	**E E T S T A**

DOWN

1	IDEA	**T H U T O G H**
2	COMPONENT	**N E M T E E L**
3	FREQUENTS	**A T S H U N**
4	TRIANGULAR PART	**A L B E G**

MYSTERY ANSWER: ☐☐☐☐☐☐☐☐☐☐

CLUE: **Biblical character who lived a long time.**

GOD CALMS FEARS

Complete the crossword puzzle by looking at the clues and unscrambling the answers. When the puzzle is complete, unscramble the circled letters to solve the Mystery Answer.

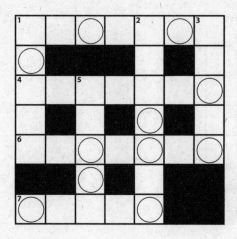

Give all your worries and cares to God, for he cares about you.

1 PETER 5:7

ACROSS

1	MADE ONE'S OWN	D A T D O P E
4	EXPOSES	S E R L A V E
6	CHILLY SEASONS	W E R T S I N
7	EGG SITES	S T E N S

DOWN

1	CUPID'S ACCESSORY	R O W R A
2	JOURNEYS	L E R S T V A
3	SPINE SUPPORTS	S K I D S
5	SECOND PLANET	S N U V E

MYSTERY ANSWER:

CLUE: God's peace calms this.

GOD IS ALWAYS WITH US

Complete the crossword puzzle by looking at the clues and unscrambling the answers. When the puzzle is complete, unscramble the circled letters to solve the Mystery Answer.

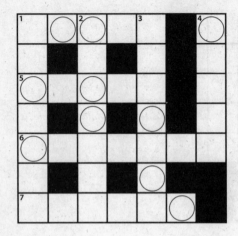

[Jesus said,] "Be sure of this: I am with you always, even to the end of the age."
MATTHEW 28:20

ACROSS

1 MELODIC SOUNDS — **M I S C U**

5 DANDY — **L E W S L**

6 COMES INTO VIEW — **P A P R E A S**

7 MOST SENIOR — **S L E E D T**

DOWN

1 MEANING — **M A S G E E S**

2 STRODE — **P E D T E P S**

3 NABS — **L O R L A S C**

4 *HAMLET* AND *MACBETH* — **A P Y S L**

MYSTERY ANSWER:

CLUE: Upper-room meal.

GOD IS OUR HEAVENLY FATHER

Complete the crossword puzzle by looking at the clues and unscrambling the answers. When the puzzle is complete, unscramble the circled letters to solve the Mystery Answer.

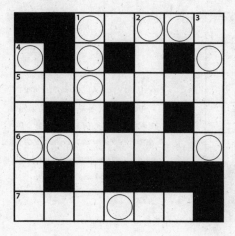

You parents—if your children ask for a loaf of bread, do you give them a stone instead? Or if they ask for a fish, do you give them a snake? Of course not! So if you sinful people know how to give good gifts to your children, how much more will your heavenly Father give good gifts to those who ask him.

MATTHEW 7:9-11

ACROSS

1	ABILITY	LILSK
5	BOOKWORMS	DREESAR
6	TRENDY	PAPLURO
7	ENCUMBER	DASLED

DOWN

1	LOST IT	APENDPS
2	PERFECT SCENARIO	ILEAD
3	LAST-PLACE FINISHER	ROSEL
4	WINE FRUIT	SEPGAR

MYSTERY ANSWER:

CLUE: **Wanderer who received abundant blessings from his father.**

GOD REMOVES DISGRACE

Complete the crossword puzzle by looking at the clues and unscrambling the answers. When the puzzle is complete, unscramble the circled letters to solve the Mystery Answer.

Fear not; you will no longer live in shame. Don't be afraid; there is no more disgrace for you. You will no longer remember the shame of your youth and the sorrows of widowhood.

ISAIAH 54:4

ACROSS

1	LUXURY CRUISER	H A T Y C
4	LABORER	K O R N M A W
6	DISEASE	S I L S L E N
7	NILE SETTING	G E T Y P

DOWN

2	REMARK	M O N T M E C
3	TWEAKS	N U E S T
4	EVEN AS	W E L H I
5	PASS ON	A E R Y L

MYSTERY ANSWER:

CLUE: The Lord's response to our weaknesses.

GOD IS OUR KNOWABLE CREATOR

Complete the crossword puzzle by looking at the clues and unscrambling the answers. When the puzzle is complete, unscramble the circled letters to solve the Mystery Answer.

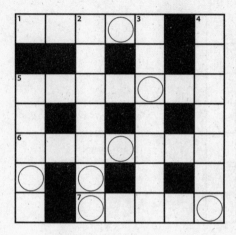

I will walk among you; I will be your God, and you will be my people.
LEVITICUS 26:12

ACROSS

1	PHYSICAL EXERTION	R O B A L
5	ROYAL RESIDENCES	E A P C A L S
6	TIP	I N P O R T E
7	SIGNAL CONVERTER	O M M E D

DOWN

2	BRUSSELS LOCATION	B U M G I E L
3	SPOKE FROM MEMORY	C R E T E D I
4	RAISED PLATFORM	S O R R T U M
5	ORGAN ELEMENTS	E S P P I

MYSTERY ANSWER:

CLUE: We can _____ with our Creator.

GOD STRENGTHENS US

Complete the crossword puzzle by looking at the clues and unscrambling the answers. When the puzzle is complete, unscramble the circled letters to solve the Mystery Answer.

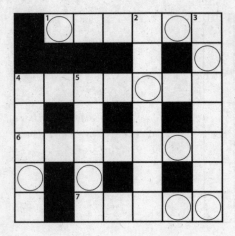

I can do everything through Christ, who gives me strength.

PHILIPPIANS 4:13

ACROSS

1 ENDURE   **F R U S E F**

4 IN SUCCESSION   **N U G N I R N**

6 FRAGRANT SPRAY   **P U M E F E R**

7 STILETTOS   **L E H E S**

DOWN

2 FIASCO   **U I F R E L A**

3 MANIPULATORS   **G E R R S I G**

4 ANSWER   **R Y P E L**

5 POLE OR STAR   **T R O H N**

MYSTERY ANSWER:

CLUE: Extent of God's power.

GOD STEERS US FROM TEMPTATION

Complete the crossword puzzle by looking at the clues and unscrambling the answers. When the puzzle is complete, unscramble the circled letters to solve the Mystery Answer.

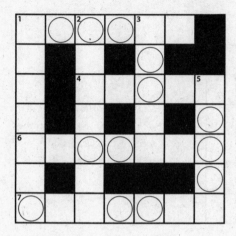

Since [Christ] himself has gone through suffering and testing, he is able to help us when we are being tested.
HEBREWS 2:18

ACROSS

1 REDUCES TO PIECES   **B A S R K E**

4 PROTRUSIONS   **B O N K S**

6 VAST   **E M M N E S I**

7 EXPRESSIVE MOVEMENT   **G R E E S T U**

DOWN

1 MURMURING   **Z I B U N G Z**

2 IGLOO DWELLERS   **I M E S O K S**

3 NOTORIOUS   **W O N N K**

5 MOVIE CLIP   **E N S E C**

MYSTERY ANSWER:

CLUE: The Lord gives us this to keep us from temptation and trouble.

GOD IS PLEASED BY OUR GOOD WORKS

Complete the crossword puzzle by looking at the clues and unscrambling the answers. When the puzzle is complete, unscramble the circled letters to solve the Mystery Answer.

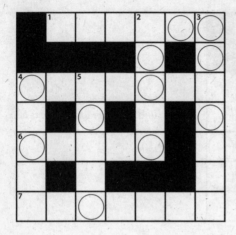

Don't forget to do good and to share with those in need. These are the sacrifices that please God.
HEBREWS 13:16

ACROSS

1	PINNACLE	**S M U T I M**
4	CROWDED TOGETHER	**D U D H E D L**
6	BELLY	**M U T Y M**
7	MERIT	**R E D E V E S**

DOWN

2	OPAQUE	**K I M L Y**
3	EARLY FROG	**A L D O P T E**
4	ABHORRENT	**D H E T A**
5	INDOOR STADIUMS	**S E O M D**

MYSTERY ANSWER:

CLUE: Gracious servanthood toward others.

GOD NOURISHES SOULS

Complete the crossword puzzle by looking at the clues and unscrambling the answers. When the puzzle is complete, unscramble the circled letters to solve the Mystery Answer.

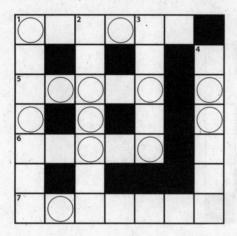

Your kindness will reward you, but your cruelty will destroy you.

PROVERBS 11:17

ACROSS

1	LESSEN	DUCEER
5	CONSTRAIN	TILMI
6	DECIMAL	HETTN
7	AVERSION	ISELKID

DOWN

1	AKIN	TALREED
2	DICTATES	SMADDEN
3	CLUTCH	HACCT
4	SNARL	GLATEN

MYSTERY ANSWER:

CLUE: One who shows kindness to those in need.

GOD FORGIVES

Complete the crossword puzzle by looking at the clues and unscrambling the answers. When the puzzle is complete, unscramble the circled letters to solve the Mystery Answer.

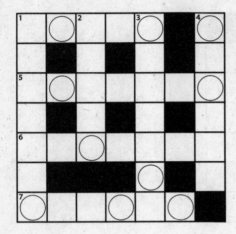

If you forgive those who sin against you, your heavenly Father will forgive you.

MATTHEW 6:14

ACROSS

1	GASEOUS PARTICLES	**V O R A P**
5	HOT WATER	**E U R B L O T**
6	VERY LARGE	**I M V E S A S**
7	ZIP	**H U N T A G**

DOWN

1	DIETARY ESSENTIAL	**V A I N M I T**
2	PUTS TOGETHER	**O P S L O**
3	DEBRIS	**H U B I R B S**
4	PLAY PARTS	**N E C E S S**

MYSTERY ANSWER:

CLUE: **Violate a commandment.**

GOD HELPS US LIVE IN PEACE

Complete the crossword puzzle by looking at the clues and unscrambling the answers. When the puzzle is complete, unscramble the circled letters to solve the Mystery Answer.

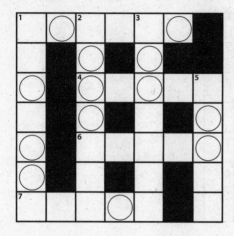

When people's lives please the LORD, even their enemies are at peace with them.

PROVERBS 16:7

ACROSS

1	LOADED	**K A D P E C**
4	ENCHANTING	**G A M C I**
6	CABLES	**D R O C S**
7	BRACKISH	**T Y L S A**

DOWN

1	CLERGYMEN	**R A N S O P S**
2	SIDESPLITTING	**L I C C O A M**
3	ENTHUSIASTICALLY	**E Y E G L A R**
5	BOXES	**E C A S S**

MYSTERY ANSWER:

CLUE: One who acted peacefully toward an enemy.

GOD PROVIDES POWER

Complete the crossword puzzle by looking at the clues and unscrambling the answers. When the puzzle is complete, unscramble the circled letters to solve the Mystery Answer.

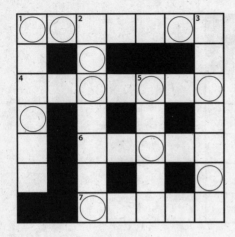

With God's help we will do mighty things, for he will trample down our foes.

PSALM 108:13

ACROSS

1	TAKES OFF	**S T R E E D S**
4	SOLUTIONS	**W A R N E S S**
6	WIPE OUT	**R E E S A**
7	SOCIAL OUTINGS	**T E A D S**

DOWN

1	HEARTFELT	**L A Y E R D**
2	PUT ON HOLD	**P E S N U D S**
3	TECHNIQUES	**M E S S T Y S**
5	PRECISE	**X E C A T**

MYSTERY ANSWER: ⬜⬜⬜⬜⬜⬜⬜ ⬜⬜⬜⬜

CLUE: Size of faith to move mountains.

GOD PERMITS CONSEQUENCES
FOR OUR ACTIONS

Complete the crossword puzzle by looking at the clues and unscrambling the answers. When the puzzle is complete, unscramble the circled letters to solve the Mystery Answer.

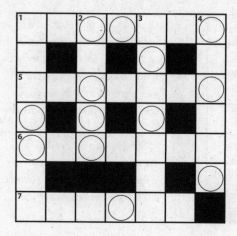

Those who love pleasure become poor; those who love wine and luxury will never be rich.
PROVERBS 21:17

ACROSS

1	HAIRBREADTH	EISHWKR
5	LENDS AN EAR	LENISST
6	GAP	PEONGIN
7	VIGOR	RENGEY

DOWN

1	GREETING	WEEMLOC
2	TOPIC	SEUIS
3	CUSTODY	GIEPENK
4	QUIT	SIGREN

MYSTERY ANSWER:

CLUE: Sinful behavior always has _____.

GOD IS NEAR

Complete the crossword puzzle by looking at the clues and unscrambling the answers. When the puzzle is complete, unscramble the circled letters to solve the Mystery Answer.

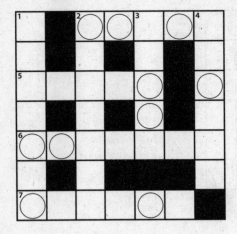

O Jacob, listen to the LORD who created you. O Israel, the one who formed you says, "Do not be afraid, for I have ransomed you. I have called you by name; you are mine. When you go through deep waters, I will be with you. When you go through rivers of difficulty, you will not drown. When you walk through the fire of oppression, you will not be burned up; the flames will not consume you."
ISAIAH 43:1-2

ACROSS

2	YOUNGSTER	DILCH
5	WORK FOR	REVES
6	GOBLETS	SALSEGS
7	DUSK	ETNUSS

DOWN

1	PLANS	NESSDIG
2	DRAPE	CAURINT
3	THOUGHTS	EDAIS
4	BREAKFAST PASTRY	IDNASH

MYSTERY ANSWER:

CLUE: The Lord's presence helps us face our _____.

GOD KEEPS US ACCOUNTABLE

Complete the crossword puzzle by looking at the clues and unscrambling the answers. When the puzzle is complete, unscramble the circled letters to solve the Mystery Answer.

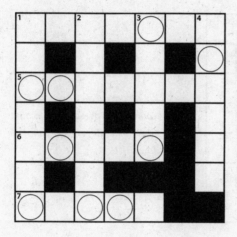

If you are faithful in little things, you will be faithful in large ones. But if you are dishonest in little things, you won't be honest with greater responsibilities.

LUKE 16:10

ACROSS

1	BACK TO THE BUFFET	ENDCOSS
5	CIRCLING	GINNGIR
6	EUROPEAN "BOOT"	ILYAT
7	SLALOM MARKERS	SAGET

DOWN

1	CREATING PILES	SNIRGOT
2	ELECTRICAL JUNCTION	TACTONC
3	LOUD	ISOYN
4	TRAFFIC LIGHT	GLISAN

MYSTERY ANSWER:

CLUE: Faithful responsibility.

GOD HONORS THE RIGHTEOUS

Complete the crossword puzzle by looking at the clues and unscrambling the answers. When the puzzle is complete, unscramble the circled letters to solve the Mystery Answer.

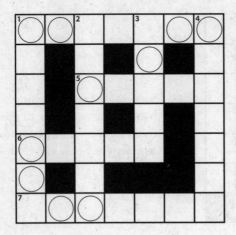

"Abraham believed God, and God counted him as righteous because of his faith." He was even called the friend of God.
JAMES 2:23

ACROSS

1	LAUDED	**S P A R D I E**
5	BROADWAY PRODUCTIONS	**W H O S S**
6	YOUNG HORSES	**O L A F S**
7	BIG SCREENS	**S E M C I A N**

DOWN

1	CONCILIATORY	**C A F I P I C**
2	REFRAIN	**B A S T I N A**
3	BOUTIQUES	**S P O S H**
4	CONFER	**D U S S I C S**

MYSTERY ANSWER:

CLUE: Our _____ with God was restored by Christ's death.

GOD EMBRACES US AS FAMILY

Complete the crossword puzzle by looking at the clues and unscrambling the answers. When the puzzle is complete, unscramble the circled letters to solve the Mystery Answer.

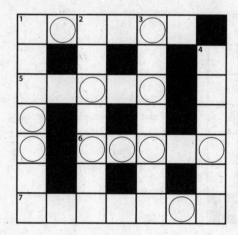

To all who believed him and accepted him, he gave the right to become children of God.

JOHN 1:12

ACROSS

1	STAY	RENMIA
5	ADJUST	TAPAD
6	INTERIOR	NERIN
7	COLD POINTS	GEDERES

DOWN

1	EXTENDED	CEHARDE
2	DEFINITION	EGAMINN
3	EXTREME	NEENTIS
4	REALIZES	NELSRA

MYSTERY ANSWER:

CLUE: **Generational legacy.**

GOD SUSTAINS DURING FAMINE

Complete the crossword puzzle by looking at the clues and unscrambling the answers. When the puzzle is complete, unscramble the circled letters to solve the Mystery Answer.

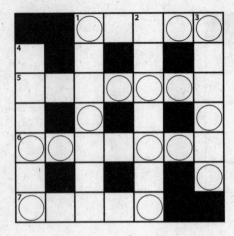

The LORD watches over those who fear him, those who rely on his unfailing love. He rescues them from death and keeps them alive in times of famine.
PSALM 33:18-19

ACROSS

1	LIKE A DUNCE CAP	N O C C I
5	COLORIST	T I N E A R P
6	ATTEMPTS	F R E S F O T
7	MONARCHIC	R Y L O A

DOWN

1	MOST IMPORTANTLY	C Y H I L F E
2	INBORN	T R A U L A N
3	GENTLE TOUCH	S E R C A S
4	SHOW UP	R E A P P A

MYSTERY ANSWER:

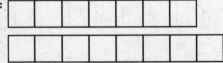

CLUE: Abundant region where the Garden of Eden may have been located.

GOD BLESSES THE FAITHFUL

Complete the crossword puzzle by looking at the clues and unscrambling the answers. When the puzzle is complete, unscramble the circled letters to solve the Mystery Answer.

The trustworthy person will get a rich reward, but a person who wants quick riches will get into trouble.
PROVERBS 28:20

ACROSS

1 SPECTACLE — **T H I G S**

4 HANGMAN'S TOOL — **E O S O N**

6 UFO TRAVELER — **I L N E A**

7 FOES — **E I M E E N S**

DOWN

1 PORK LINK — **A G U E S S A**

2 AUTHENTIC — **N E G I E N U**

3 IRRITATION — **T R O H N**

5 SIDES — **G E E D S**

MYSTERY ANSWER:

CLUE: Through faith God can move _____.

GOD GIVES NEW BEGINNINGS

Complete the crossword puzzle by looking at the clues and unscrambling the answers. When the puzzle is complete, unscramble the circled letters to solve the Mystery Answer.

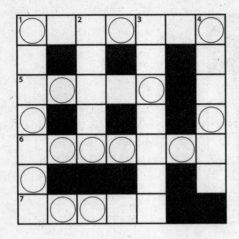

He has removed our sins as far from us as the east is from the west.

PSALM 103:12

ACROSS

1	SLOPING LETTERS	C L I A T I S
5	DEMONSTRATED	W H O N S
6	MORE LUCID	R A C E L E R
7	USE UP	S N E P D

DOWN

1	BUGS	N E S C I S T
2	EMERGED FROM DREAMLAND	A W E K O
3	UNNOTICED	O R N I D G E
4	BASE PAY	A Y L S A R

MYSTERY ANSWER:

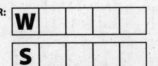
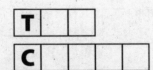

CLUE: What Christ does when we ask for forgiveness.

GOD REWARDS HUMILITY

Complete the crossword puzzle by looking at the clues and unscrambling the answers. When the puzzle is complete, unscramble the circled letters to solve the Mystery Answer.

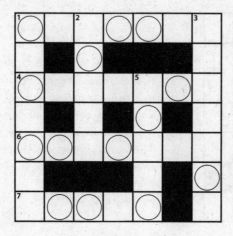

Humble yourselves, therefore, under God's mighty hand, that he may lift you up in due time.
1 PETER 5:6, NIV

ACROSS

1	CONDIMENT	**H U C K T E P**
4	ELECTRIC CAR	**L O R Y E L T**
6	KIDNAP VICTIM	**A S E O G H T**
7	HOSPITAL EMPLOYEE	**R E S U N**

DOWN

1	MEALTIME LOCATION	**N I C K T H E**
2	JOGGING GAITS	**R O T T S**
3	FEE	**M A T Y N E P**
5	DEPART	**A L V E E**

MYSTERY ANSWER:

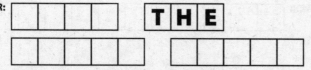

CLUE: Show humility when you are persecuted.

93

GOD DELIVERS FROM ENEMIES

Complete the crossword puzzle by looking at the clues and unscrambling the answers. When the puzzle is complete, unscramble the circled letters to solve the Mystery Answer.

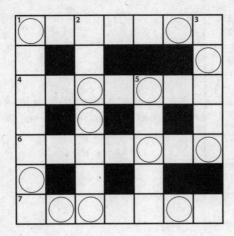

The LORD lives! Praise to my Rock! May the God of my salvation be exalted! He is the God who pays back those who harm me; he subdues the nations under me and rescues me from my enemies. You hold me safe beyond the reach of my enemies; you save me from violent opponents.
PSALM 18:46-48

ACROSS

1	MORE UNCLEAN	**TIERRID**
4	COMMENTS	**MEKARRS**
6	OVERRUNS	**VIDENAS**
7	RACES	**LOGLAPS**

DOWN

1	PETER PAN CLAN	**GLARDIN**
2	EJECTION	**AVMELOR**
3	ASCENDS	**IRESS**
5	WIRELESS	**ARODI**

MYSTERY ANSWER:

CLUE: Israelite destination.

GOD HAS COMPASSION
FOR YOUR SORROWS

Complete the crossword puzzle by looking at the clues and unscrambling the answers. When the puzzle is complete, unscramble the circled letters to solve the Mystery Answer.

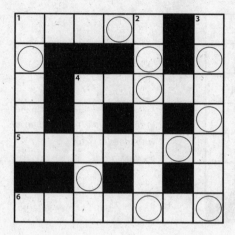

You keep track of all my sorrows. You have collected all my tears in your bottle. You have recorded each one in your book.

PSALM 56:8

ACROSS

1	THREE DIMENSIONAL	**B U C C I**
4	TITLE HOLDER	**E W O R N**
5	NEW YORK BILLS	**F L O U B F A**
6	BLOOD RELATIONS	**P E R T N A S**

DOWN

1	SCALE	**B L I C M**
2	HOLD	**T O N N I A C**
3	ENTITIES	**R O S S P E N**
4	PROPOSE	**F E F R O**

MYSTERY ANSWER:

CLUE: A sorrow the Lord can relieve.

GOD PROTECTS YOU FROM PERIL

Complete the crossword puzzle by looking at the clues and unscrambling the answers. When the puzzle is complete, unscramble the circled letters to solve the Mystery Answer.

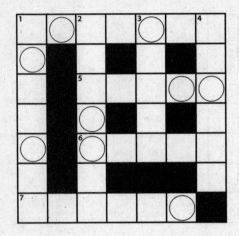

You are my hiding place; you protect me from trouble. You surround me with songs of victory.

PSALM 32:7

ACROSS

1	ADDITIONALLY	SEBISDE
5	BAGGAGE	GAROC
6	HARMONIOUS JINGLE	HEMRY
7	WHIRLPOOLS	DISEED

DOWN

1	GYMNASTICS ASSET	ALBECAN
2	STABILIZED	CUSDEER
3	CORRUPT	TYRID
4	SQUIRRELS AWAY	ERTOSS

MYSTERY ANSWER:

CLUE: God delivers his children from _____ situations.

96

GOD IS NEAR

Complete the crossword puzzle by looking at the clues and unscrambling the answers. When the puzzle is complete, unscramble the circled letters to solve the Mystery Answer.

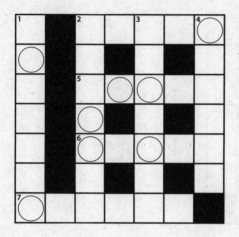

The Lord replied, "I will personally go with you, Moses, and I will give you rest."

EXODUS 33:14

ACROSS

2 CLEAR FLUID   **R E M U S**

5 LINED   **L E D U R**

6 ESSENTIALS   **N E S E D**

7 POWERFUL PERSON   **E S T R A M**

DOWN

1 MEDIEVAL ESTATE   **M O E D I F F**

2 INDIVIDUAL HAIRS   **N T R A D S S**

3 TAKE THE EDGE OFF   **I V E L R E E**

4 PLAIN AND SIMPLE   **D O T S E M**

MYSTERY ANSWER: ☐☐☐☐☐☐☐☐

CLUE: "God is with us."

GOD PROVIDES REDEMPTION

Complete the crossword puzzle by looking at the clues and unscrambling the answers. When the puzzle is complete, unscramble the circled letters to solve the Mystery Answer.

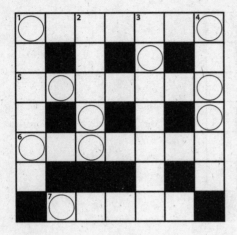

Riches won't help on the day of judgment, but right living can save you from death.

PROVERBS 11:4

ACROSS

1	PUMPKIN HABITATS	**C A P S E T H**
5	GEAR	**G L A G U E G**
6	PORTION	**R E N G I V S**
7	CONTINUES	**A T S Y S**

DOWN

1	REFINE	**O H S L I P**
2	WOODS ON THE GREEN	**G R E T I**
3	WITH GREAT WEIGHT	**V A Y L E I H**
4	BIG HAMMER	**G E S D E L**

MYSTERY ANSWER:

CLUE: Righteousness _____ riches.

GOD WILL BE EXALTED AROUND THE WORLD

Complete the crossword puzzle by looking at the clues and unscrambling the answers. When the puzzle is complete, unscramble the circled letters to solve the Mystery Answer.

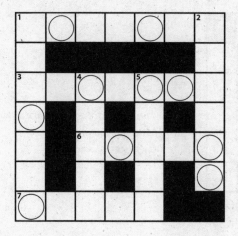

Be still and know that I am God; I will be exalted among the nations, I will be exalted in the earth.

PSALM 46:10, NIV

ACROSS

1 FUNNY   G U M I N A S

3 REFURBISH   S E R R T O E

6 STORAGE SHELVES   C K R S A

7 MORE RECENT   W E R E N

DOWN

1 EGYPTIAN OR ETHIOPIAN   C A I N A R F

2 OILY   R Y E G A S

4 FASTENER   S W E R C

5 HAPPEN   C O U R C

MYSTERY ANSWER:

CLUE: One who declares Christ to the nations.

GOD RESPONDS TO OUR FAITH

Complete the crossword puzzle by looking at the clues and unscrambling the answers. When the puzzle is complete, unscramble the circled letters to solve the Mystery Answer.

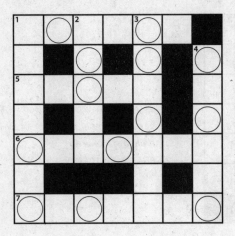

You can pray for anything, and if you have faith, you will receive it.

MATTHEW 21:22

ACROSS

1	TINTS	SCLORO
5	SKINS	SIRND
6	HOME NUMBER	DESDARS
7	EVERY EVENING	HIGLYNT

DOWN

1	SHADE	TARNIUC
2	WRINKLED	IDLEN
3	REVERE	SCREEPT
4	SOGGY	RYHAMS

MYSTERY ANSWER:

CLUE: A great way to start your day.

GOD WILL ALWAYS BE WITH YOU

Complete the crossword puzzle by looking at the clues and unscrambling the answers. When the puzzle is complete, unscramble the circled letters to solve the Mystery Answer.

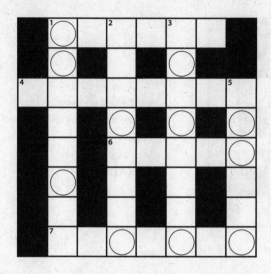

Where can I go from your Spirit? Where can I flee from your presence?
PSALM 139:7, NIV

ACROSS

1 SPLENDOR — YUBAET

4 FAVOR — SINSDENK

6 SAMPLE — SETTA

7 BEASTS OF BURDEN — SKYNODE

DOWN

1 WHITEOUT — ZIRZBALD

2 MATH FUNCTION — DIDION.TA.

3 PIRATE'S PLUNDER — REETARUS

5 EXHAUSTS — DEPSSN

MYSTERY ANSWER:

CLUE: Always together, never apart.

GOD ALLEVIATES PAIN

Complete the crossword puzzle by looking at the clues and unscrambling the answers. When the puzzle is complete, unscramble the circled letters to solve the Mystery Answer.

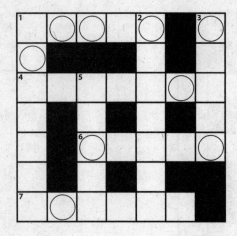

He will wipe every tear from their eyes, and there will be no more death or sorrow or crying or pain. All these things are gone forever.

REVELATION 21:4

ACROSS

1   MOST UNFAVORABLE   **T R O W S**

4   FLUIDS   **U L D I S I Q**

6   SPRITES   **L E S E V**

7   FAT   **R A E G E S**

DOWN

1   STROLLING   **K N A W G L I**

2   SHOPLIFTERS   **V E E T H I S**

3   MASQUERADES   **P E S S O**

5   LINE   **E E Q U U**

MYSTERY ANSWER:

CLUE: **These will be absent on the new earth.**

GOD IS GOOD TO ALL

Complete the crossword puzzle by looking at the clues and unscrambling the answers. When the puzzle is complete, unscramble the circled letters to solve the Mystery Answer.

The LORD is good to everyone. He showers compassion on all his creation. All of your works will thank you, LORD, and your faithful followers will praise you.

PSALM 145:9-10

ACROSS

2	MUGGERS	**BRESBRO**
5	ADJUSTING	**GAPNAIDT**
6	WOUND REPAIRS	**TECSITHS**
7	VASTLY	**ILHYGH**

DOWN

1	UPRIGHT	**VALCRIET**
2	BELLOWS	**ORRSA**
3	AFLAME	**BLIZNAG**
4	SOLOIST	**RINEGS**

MYSTERY ANSWER:

CLUE: Jubilation for the Lord's goodness.

GOD INSTILLS PEACE

Complete the crossword puzzle by looking at the clues and unscrambling the answers. When the puzzle is complete, unscramble the circled letters to solve the Mystery Answer.

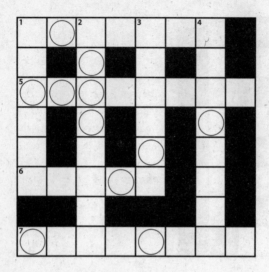

The Lᴏʀᴅ bless you and keep you; the Lᴏʀᴅ make his face shine upon you and be gracious to you; the Lᴏʀᴅ turn his face toward you and give you peace.
NUMBERS 6:24-26, NIV

ACROSS

1 ADORATION — **SHOPRIW**

5 BAKING MEASUREMENT — **POTAOSNE**

6 BEE ASSAULT — **SNIGT**

7 DEFEAT — **NOSQETUC**

DOWN

1 HOSES — **STAREW**

2 RESPONSE — **NAECOTIR**

3 WISHING — **GOPNIH**

4 SUBSTITUTE WORDS — **ROONNUPS**

MYSTERY ANSWER:

CLUE: The Lord's _____ is full of grace and peace.

GOD WILL KEEP HIS PROMISES

Complete the crossword puzzle by looking at the clues and unscrambling the answers. When the puzzle is complete, unscramble the circled letters to solve the Mystery Answer.

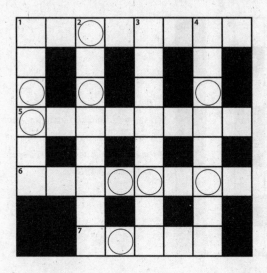

Your promises have been thoroughly tested; that is why I love them so much.

PSALM 119:140

ACROSS

1	FINISHES CHEWING	**W O L S L A W S**
5	FRUIT FIELDS	**D O R C A R S H**
6	TRAIN STOPS	**N A I T O S S T**
7	GIVES UP THE GAME	**K N S T A**

DOWN

1	UTENSILS	**N O P O S S**
2	BLACKHAWK OR APACHE	**C A F A R I R T**
3	SITE	**T I N A L O C O**
4	NUPTIALS	**G W I N D D E S**

MYSTERY ANSWER:

CLUE: Our response to God's faithfulness.

GOD WILL DELIVER ON HIS INTENTIONS

Complete the crossword puzzle by looking at the clues and unscrambling the answers. When the puzzle is complete, unscramble the circled letters to solve the Mystery Answer.

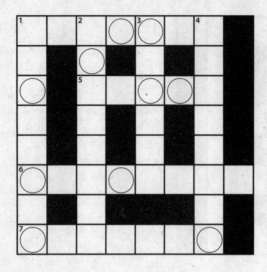

I make known the end from the beginning, from ancient times, what is still to come. I say: My purpose will stand, and I will do all that I please.
ISAIAH 46:10, NIV

ACROSS

#	Clue	Scrambled
1	CONTACTS	SHUTCEO
5	MATADOR'S LAND	NIPSA
6	SMOKE TUBES	MYSHEINC
7	MORALS	SENOSLS

DOWN

#	Clue	Scrambled
1	SULTRY	COPTRAIL
2	SECOND LEVEL	SPIATRUS
3	BLISS	NAVEEH
4	SIMILAR MEANINGS	NYNYMOSS

MYSTERY ANSWER: ☐☐☐☐☐☐☐☐☐☐

CLUE: The Lord will _____ all of his purposes.

GOD IS A COMPASSIONATE FATHER

Complete the crossword puzzle by looking at the clues and unscrambling the answers. When the puzzle is complete, unscramble the circled letters to solve the Mystery Answer.

Jerusalem says, "The LORD has deserted us; the Lord has forgotten us." "Never! Can a mother forget her nursing child? Can she feel no love for the child she has borne? But even if that were possible, I would not forget you! See, I have written your name on the palms of my hands. Always in my mind is a picture of Jerusalem's walls in ruins."

ISAIAH 49:14-16

ACROSS

1 SURMISE   **C O N K E R**

3 REASONABLE   **B L E S S I N E**

6 TINNY   **T E L M A L C I**

7 FENS   **D O W N A L L S**

DOWN

1 LOOK LIKE   **B E E S R E L M**

2 SNACKING   **G L I N N B I B**

4 SLOW MOVER   **I N S A L**

5 PARDON   **X U E C E S**

MYSTERY ANSWER:

CLUE: **Even in the greatest trials, God's people will not face _____.**

GOD PROVIDES ENDURING LOVE

Complete the crossword puzzle by looking at the clues and unscrambling the answers. When the puzzle is complete, unscramble the circled letters to solve the Mystery Answer.

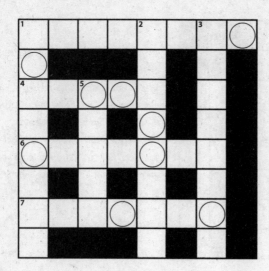

Give thanks to the Lord, for he is good!
His faithful love endures forever.
PSALM 107:1

ACROSS

1	EXPLAIN	BRISCEED
4	UP TO THE TIME	LUNIT
6	CONFIDED	SUTTDER
7	INDEFINITE	WONNUNK

DOWN

1	UNSURE	BUFLUTOD
2	FAMILY MEMBER	ELONITAR
3	PRODUCING OFFSPRING	REBENDIG
5	MAIN STEM	NURKT

MYSTERY ANSWER: ☐☐☐☐☐☐☐☐☐☐

CLUE: **What our prayers always get from God.**

GOD WILL NEVER FORSAKE YOU

Complete the crossword puzzle by looking at the clues and unscrambling the answers. When the puzzle is complete, unscramble the circled letters to solve the Mystery Answer.

*Those who know your name trust in you, for you, O L*ORD*, do not abandon those who search for you.*

PSALM 9:10

ACROSS

3	HAPHAZARDLY	W A Y N O H
5	TREE EXTENSIONS	C E N B R A S H
7	PROBES	P L E E R S O X
8	MOST CRAZY	D E W S I L T

DOWN

1	TRIFLE	B L U B E A
2	TREATISES	S H E S T E
4	EXAMINED BY TOUCH	N E D D L A H
6	PAINS	R U T H S

MYSTERY ANSWER:

CLUE: **Deserving of confidence.**

109

GOD LIFTS BURDENS

Complete the crossword puzzle by looking at the clues and unscrambling the answers. When the puzzle is complete, unscramble the circled letters to solve the Mystery Answer.

Give your burdens to the LORD, and he will take care of you. He will not permit the godly to slip and fall.
PSALM 55:22

ACROSS

1	GETS AWAY	SEEPCAS
5	THANKSGIVING DAY	DYSHARTU
6	MESMERIZING	CEGAMINT
7	DETAILED	GROOHUHT

DOWN

1	EDUCATED GUESS	MAITTSEE
2	HUNG ONTO	LUGNC
3	KINDERGARTEN GOOP	SPETA
4	TERRORIZING	RICSAGN

MYSTERY ANSWER:

CLUE: **One who gives guidance during trials.**

GOD IS A FORTRESS

Complete the crossword puzzle by looking at the clues and unscrambling the answers. When the puzzle is complete, unscramble the circled letters to solve the Mystery Answer.

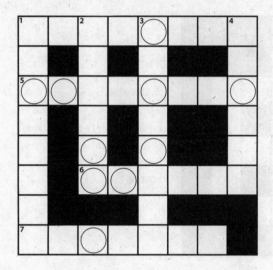

The LORD is my rock, my fortress, and my savior; my God is my rock, in whom I find protection. He is my shield, the power that saves me, and my place of safety.

PSALM 18:2

ACROSS

1 ROOTED   **H E R N C O D A**

5 FATHOMING   **D I G O N N U S**

6 RAIL RIDERS   **N I S T R A**

7 POSTPONED   **E E D D A Y L**

DOWN

1 ALLOCATED   **S E A G S N I D**

2 TRAPPED   **G U T H C A**

3 AVERAGE   **D O N Y A R I R**

4 FINGERS AND TOES   **S I D T I G**

MYSTERY ANSWER:

CLUE: **God is a mighty fortress and our _____ in times of trouble.**

GOD REWARDS THE HUMBLE

Complete the crossword puzzle by looking at the clues and unscrambling the answers. When the puzzle is complete, unscramble the circled letters to solve the Mystery Answer.

The greatest among you must be a servant. But those who exalt themselves will be humbled, and those who humble themselves will be exalted.

MATTHEW 23:11-12

ACROSS

1	ILLUMINATION DEVICES	P L A S M
4	BABY ROCKERS	S L A R D E C
6	SUMMER ACCESSORY	N A A L D S
7	LIVED THROUGH	V U S E D R I V

DOWN

1	MOST FORTUNATE	S I T U C K E L
2	INCOME	N A S E M
3	GLORIOUS	N E D D S I P L
5	TREE OFFERING	D E H A S

MYSTERY ANSWER:

CLUE: A young girl who served.

GOD WILL GIVE TO THOSE WHO SEEK HIM

Complete the crossword puzzle by looking at the clues and unscrambling the answers. When the puzzle is complete, unscramble the circled letters to solve the Mystery Answer.

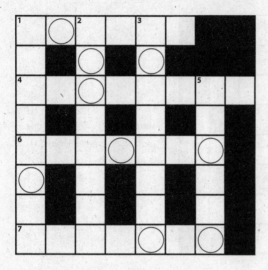

Seek first his kingdom and his righteousness, and all these things will be given to you as well. Therefore do not worry about tomorrow, for tomorrow will worry about itself. Each day has enough trouble of its own.
MATTHEW 6:33-34, NIV

ACROSS

1 KINDERGARTEN ESSENTIAL — RACNOY

4 ARMED SERVICES — RILYTAIM

6 YEARNING — NILNOGG

7 DISMISSES — EXCESUS

DOWN

1 LACKING NOTHING — PELMETOC

2 MAINE OCEAN VIEW — CALNITAT

3 SKETCHES — SOENIULT

5 SCAMPS — REUGOS

MYSTERY ANSWER: ⬜⬜⬜⬜⬜⬜⬜⬜⬜⬜

CLUE: Seek the Lord to see you through your _____.

113

GOD GIVES HOPE TO THE DESPONDENT

Complete the crossword puzzle by looking at the clues and unscrambling the answers. When the puzzle is complete, unscramble the circled letters to solve the Mystery Answer.

Why am I discouraged? Why is my heart so sad? I will put my hope in God! I will praise him again.
PSALM 42:5

ACROSS

1	CIRCUS PERFORMER	C A R B O T A
4	IN PRIVATE	C L Y T E E R S
6	ONTO DRY LAND	H E A R O S
7	PLEADED WITH	E D R U G

DOWN

1	GATHERING OF MANY PEOPLE	S L A B Y S M E
2	CULTURAL	C L A R I A
3	DESPITE	L O T G U H A H
5	DEFER	I D L E Y

MYSTERY ANSWER:

CLUE: With the Lord's help, the greatest trials become _____.

GOD WILL HELP YOU GUARD YOUR HEARTS

Complete the crossword puzzle by looking at the clues and unscrambling the answers. When the puzzle is complete, unscramble the circled letters to solve the Mystery Answer.

Do not be anxious about anything, but in everything, by prayer and petition, with thanksgiving, present your requests to God. And the peace of God, which transcends all understanding, will guard your hearts and your minds in Christ Jesus.

PHILIPPIANS 4:6-7, NIV

ACROSS

1 BASES   **TOMBOST**

4 ACKNOWLEDGMENT   **DETCIR**

5 BOTHER   **CISENNAU**

6 PRESUMED   **PODUSSEP**

DOWN

1 MONKEY CHOW   **ANNBAAS**

2 SWITCHBOARD JOCKEY   **ARETROOP**

3 TATTLES   **SCINSETH**

4 BRITTLE   **PIRCS**

MYSTERY ANSWER:

CLUE: Focus your _____ on Jesus.

GOD WATCHES OVER YOU

Complete the crossword puzzle by looking at the clues and unscrambling the answers. When the puzzle is complete, unscramble the circled letters to solve the Mystery Answer.

The eyes of the Lord search the whole earth in order to strengthen those whose hearts are fully committed to him.
2 CHRONICLES 16:9

ACROSS

1	TEMPERAMENTS	N E R S A U T
5	CLEAR	N E D T I E V
6	ABSOLVED	V O G F I R N E
7	HANGS ONTO	P E S E K

DOWN

1	COMPUTER OR SPIRAL	B E K O O N T O
2	TAXING	G Y T N I R
3	GAINS	C R E V I S E E
4	BLEACHERS	T A N G E S I

MYSTERY ANSWER: ☐☐☐☐☐☐☐☐☐☐☐☐☐

CLUE: Your heart is _____ to God.

GOD CAN RESCUE THE TROUBLED

Complete the crossword puzzle by looking at the clues and unscrambling the answers. When the puzzle is complete, unscramble the circled letters to solve the Mystery Answer.

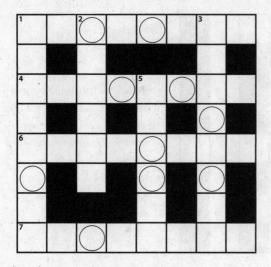

[God] grants the desires of those who fear him; he hears their cries for help and rescues them.

PSALM 145:19

ACROSS

1	BY THE BOOK	ROYPPLER
4	DRILL	CREESIXE
6	SHUDDERED	BELTEMRD
7	NEXT TO THE HIGHWAY	ODDIARES

DOWN

1	MORE ATTRACTIVE	TREEPTIR
2	COMPLIED	YODEBE
3	TOOK NOTE	EDENTILS
5	TV LINES	BELACS

MYSTERY ANSWER:

CLUE: God's provided rescue for those who fear him.

GOD GIVES CONSOLATION AND JOY

Complete the crossword puzzle by looking at the clues and unscrambling the answers. When the puzzle is complete, unscramble the circled letters to solve the Mystery Answer.

I cried out, "I am slipping!" but your unfailing love, O Lᴏʀᴅ, supported me. When doubts filled my mind, your comfort gave me renewed hope and cheer.

PSALM 94:18-19

ACROSS

1	TIME-HONORED	SCALCIS
4	CONCUR	REAGE
6	MEMORABLE	CITISHRO
7	REQUIRING	NEDGEIN

DOWN

1	WRECKING	SCINARGH
2	NABBED BY THE COPS	TEESARDR
3	BUGGY	ARGIAREC
5	FOREIGN	TECIOX

MYSTERY ANSWER:

CLUE: **The Lord relieves those who are _____.**

GOD OFFERS PERMANENT LOVE

Complete the crossword puzzle by looking at the clues and unscrambling the answers. When the puzzle is complete, unscramble the circled letters to solve the Mystery Answer.

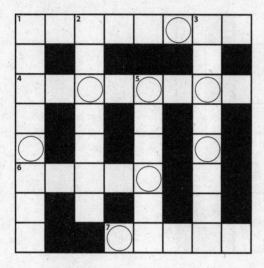

I am convinced that nothing can ever separate us from God's love. Neither death nor life, neither angels nor demons, neither our fears for today nor our worries about tomorrow—not even the powers of hell can separate us from God's love. No power in the sky above or in the earth below— indeed, nothing in all creation will ever be able to separate us from the love of God that is revealed in Christ Jesus our Lord.
ROMANS 8:38-39

ACROSS

1	CHOKER	KELNCEAC
4	SPRINKLES	LARFLIAN
6	HAPPENING	ENTEV
7	FINISH THE CAKE	STORF

DOWN

1	BOREAL	THRONENR
2	ENGLISH FIELD GAME	CITEKRC
3	GROWS IN AGAR	CURUTSEL
5	MORE STOUT	RETAFT

MYSTERY ANSWER:

CLUE: The Lord is _____ in all circumstances.

GOD EMBRACES YOU

Complete the crossword puzzle by looking at the clues and unscrambling the answers. When the puzzle is complete, unscramble the circled letters to solve the Mystery Answer.

Even if my father and mother abandon me, the LORD will hold me close.
PSALM 27:10

ACROSS

3 MORE PARCHED   **R I R E D**

4 COMMONWEALTH   **C L U P I B E R**

5 SWELLS   **B L O S O L A N**

6 OLD VACATION RECORDS   **D E S S I L**

DOWN

1 THOUSANDS OF THOUSANDS   **S O L L I M I N**

2 SETS A VALUE   **C R I S P E**

3 BENT OVER   **B O D D E L U**

4 ROYAL GARMENTS   **E R S B O**

MYSTERY ANSWER:

CLUE: God's faithfulness gives us _____ _____.

GOD WILL STAY WITH YOU

Complete the crossword puzzle by looking at the clues and unscrambling the answers. When the puzzle is complete, unscramble the circled letters to solve the Mystery Answer.

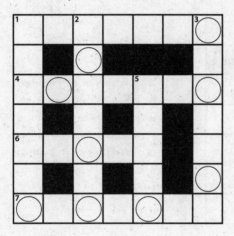

I will be your God throughout your lifetime—until your hair is white with age. I made you, and I will care for you. I will carry you along and save you.

ISAIAH 46:4

ACROSS

1 HAIR ACCESSORIES **B I N S B O R**

4 ATTACHES **N E S S A F T**

6 EIGHTEEN HOLES **D O N R U**

7 KEYED IN **T E D R E E N**

DOWN

1 ARBITRATE **F E E R E R E**

2 UNGLAZED PORCELAIN **S I T U B I C**

3 POSTPONE **P E N D U S S**

5 ONE TO RESPECT **D R E E L**

MYSTERY ANSWER:

CLUE: God is our provider and our _____.

GOD REPAYS GOOD WORKS

Complete the crossword puzzle by looking at the clues and unscrambling the answers. When the puzzle is complete, unscramble the circled letters to solve the Mystery Answer.

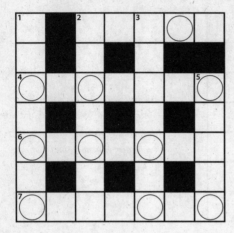

When you put on a luncheon or a banquet, . . . invite the poor, the crippled, the lame, and the blind. Then at the resurrection of the righteous, God will reward you for inviting those who could not repay you.

LUKE 14:12-14

ACROSS

2	STRONG CORDS	**S P E R O**
4	MAILING	**G E N N S I D**
6	LEFT OUT	**T I M O D E T**
7	WITH VIGOR	**G A R Y E L E**

DOWN

1	BRING BACK	**O R S T E E R**
2	ENCIRCLING	**G I N N G I R**
3	WALL COATER	**I P R E A N T**
5	LIGHTHEARTED	**D Y D I G**

MYSTERY ANSWER:

CLUE: Your _____ will be repaid.

GOD OFFERS FREEDOM FROM FEAR

Complete the crossword puzzle by looking at the clues and unscrambling the answers. When the puzzle is complete, unscramble the circled letters to solve the Mystery Answer.

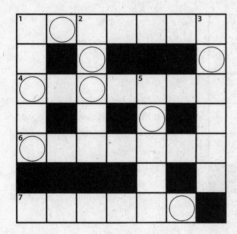

Say to those with fearful hearts, "Be strong, and do not fear, for your God is coming to destroy your enemies. He is coming to save you."

ISAIAH 35:4

ACROSS

1 STRUCK OBLIQUELY   **C A N G E L D**

4 ABANDON   **R E D F O E M**

6 CONFERENCE   **O S S E N I S**

7 PERMANENTLY   **Y A S L A W**

DOWN

1 ENDOWS   **F I G S T**

2 SECTIONS   **R A A S E**

3 NECESSITY   **M A D D E N**

5 RAYED FLOWER   **A Y S I D**

MYSTERY ANSWER:

CLUE: Your demeanor when God is by your side.

GOD PROSPERS HIS OWN

Complete the crossword puzzle by looking at the clues and unscrambling the answers. When the puzzle is complete, unscramble the circled letters to solve the Mystery Answer.

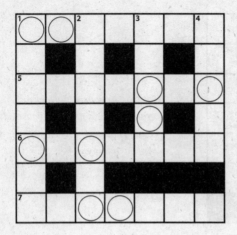

"I know the plans I have for you," says the LORD. "They are plans for good and not for disaster, to give you a future and a hope."

JEREMIAH 29:11

ACROSS

1 CREDIT CARD — CITPALS

5 CITRUS PIECE — OCTNISE

6 WITHOUT PURPOSE — SUSSLEE

7 BLOG POSTS — RITNESE

DOWN

1 GRAZING GROUND — EASTRUP

2 SOME PYRAMIDS — CENNAIT

3 NATIVE COMMUNITY — ERTBI

4 VISUAL RECEPTORS — OCSEN

MYSTERY ANSWER:

CLUE: Plan for building.

GOD CREATES HEAVENLY HOMES

Complete the crossword puzzle by looking at the clues and unscrambling the answers. When the puzzle is complete, unscramble the circled letters to solve the Mystery Answer.

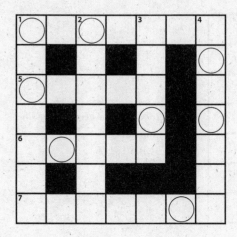

*In my Father's house are many rooms;
if it were not so, I would have told you.
I am going there to prepare a place
for you.*
JOHN 14:2, NIV

ACROSS

1	EINSTEIN'S LOVE	NICCEES
5	TOPPLE	PUSTE
6	ALARM	REDDA
7	ITEMS	TELISAD

DOWN

1	MEASURED DEPTHS	ODDENUS
2	SCRUTINIZE	NEPCIST
3	CELEBRATED	NEDOT
4	LETS OFF	UXCEESS

MYSTERY ANSWER: ⬜⬜⬜⬜⬜⬜⬜⬜⬜

CLUE: Heavenly amenities.

GOD PROMISES WE WILL NEVER BE ALONE

Complete the crossword puzzle by looking at the clues and unscrambling the answers. When the puzzle is complete, unscramble the circled letters to solve the Mystery Answer.

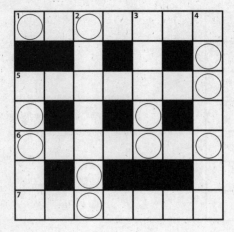

I am not alone because the Father is with me.

JOHN 16:32

ACROSS

1	UNCONCEALED	**DOXEEPS**
5	RAM	**GOSTREA**
6	ZEROS	**GUNTSHA**
7	SNIFFED	**DEMSELL**

DOWN

2	EMIT	**PEDUCOR**
3	DESTROY	**HMASS**
4	PUT ON CLOTHING	**DESERDS**
5	DESCENDS	**NISKS**

MYSTERY ANSWER:

CLUE: God's constant companionship.

GOD DIRECTS HIS OWN

Complete the crossword puzzle by looking at the clues and unscrambling the answers. When the puzzle is complete, unscramble the circled letters to solve the Mystery Answer.

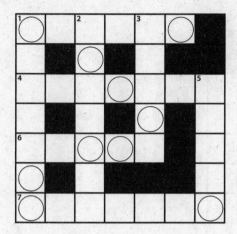

Trust in the LORD with all your heart; do not depend on your own understanding. Seek his will in all you do, and he will show you which path to take.

PROVERBS 3:5-6

ACROSS

1	UNDERGROUND	TERSCE
4	PUT OUT	DANYONE
6	DANCE MOVE	SWTTI
7	TRACKING	GONDIGG

DOWN

1	REACTED	DETTRAS
2	ASTUTE	GUNNCIN
3	PYRAMID PLACE	TEGPY
5	ELIMINATE ERRORS	BUDGE

MYSTERY ANSWER:

CLUE: Follow these when plotting your course.

GOD IS FAITHFUL

Complete the crossword puzzle by looking at the clues and unscrambling the answers. When the puzzle is complete, unscramble the circled letters to solve the Mystery Answer.

If we are unfaithful, [Christ] remains faithful, for he cannot deny who he is.
2 TIMOTHY 2:13

ACROSS

1	SIDE TABLE	WYLOOB
4	MOLDED PIECE	SCAGNIT
6	SPECIAL OCCASION	TENEV
7	SWEET TREATS	DEANUSS

DOWN

1	TRACES	COSTELA
2	JOHN WAYNE FILM	TREWENS
3	SHEEPISH	VENIO
5	SLALOM MARKERS	TEGAS

MYSTERY ANSWER:

CLUE: You can trust in God's _____ faithfulness.

GOD IS A LOVING FATHER

Complete the crossword puzzle by looking at the clues and unscrambling the answers. When the puzzle is complete, unscramble the circled letters to solve the Mystery Answer.

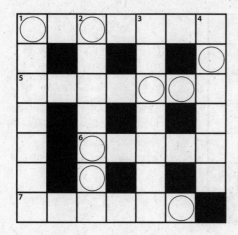

The Lord is like a father to his children, tender and compassionate to those who fear him.

PSALM 103:13

ACROSS

1 LEFT ON THE HOOK   G A N N I G H

5 OPPORTUNITY LAND   C A M E A R I

6 FIND OUT   N A R E L

7 HUFFED   S E P D A G

DOWN

1 COURT APPEARANCE   N I A R E G H

2 STITCHERS WITH EYES   L E E N S E D

3 PRETEND TO BE   M E A T I T I

4 SAND UNITS   A N G I R S

MYSTERY ANSWER:

CLUE: When we follow God, we become one of his _____.

GOD BLESSES GODLY WOMEN

Complete the crossword puzzle by looking at the clues and unscrambling the answers. When the puzzle is complete, unscramble the circled letters to solve the Mystery Answer.

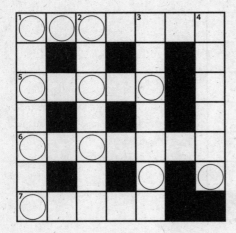

Charm is deceptive, and beauty does not last; but a woman who fears the LORD will be greatly praised.

PROVERBS 31:30

ACROSS

1	FIELD GOALS	TEBKASS
5	INSINCERE	LEAFS
6	FAUNA	ALISNAM
7	MUST	HOGUT

DOWN

1	BAFFLE	FLABOUF
2	GETTING RID OF	LENSLIG
3	GRACEFUL	LENGATE
4	SUMMER OR WINTER	HUSSAQ

MYSTERY ANSWER:

CLUE: Being godly is more important than being _____.

130

GOD CAN HELP US
LIVE WITHOUT WANT

Complete the crossword puzzle by looking at the clues and unscrambling the answers. When the puzzle is complete, unscramble the circled letters to solve the Mystery Answer.

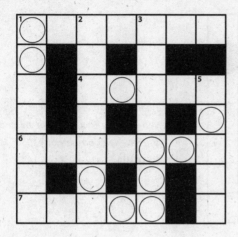

The LORD is my shepherd; I have all that I need.

PSALM 23:1

ACROSS

1	SINCE	SEACUBE
4	DEED	LITTE
6	MONITORS	DILRASZ
7	BEACHLIKE	NYADS

DOWN

1	FRAYS	BLASTET
2	NATIONAL	NIZTICE
3	UNRESERVEDLY	TYRELTU
5	PICASSO'S STAND	SEALE

MYSTERY ANSWER:

CLUE: God's plentiful provision.

GOD CAN GRANT LONG LIFE

Complete the crossword puzzle by looking at the clues and unscrambling the answers. When the puzzle is complete, unscramble the circled letters to solve the Mystery Answer.

Honor your father and mother. Then you will live a long, full life in the land the LORD your God is giving you.
EXODUS 20:12

ACROSS

1 DIPLOMAT'S DIGS   Y E S B A M S

4 TRAIN AND FIRE   N E S I G E N

6 ON A PAR WITH   L A Q U E

7 REACHES OUT   D E N S T E X

DOWN

1 CARRY OUT   C E T U X E E

2 MOST IMPOSING   G I B T E G S

3 A USE FOR ALOE   B U N N U R S

5 TRANSACTIONS   L A S S E

MYSTERY ANSWER:

CLUE: Long lifers.

132

GOD BLESSES OUR GIVING

Complete the crossword puzzle by looking at the clues and unscrambling the answers. When the puzzle is complete, unscramble the circled letters to solve the Mystery Answer.

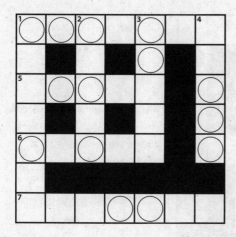

Give, and you will receive. Your gift will return to you in full—pressed down, shaken together to make room for more, running over, and poured into your lap. The amount you give will determine the amount you get back.
LUKE 6:38

ACROSS

1	INCISIVE	E P I D O N T
5	BOP OR TAP	C E N A D
6	GREAT	G L E R A
7	CREATED	V I D S E D E

DOWN

1	STEERED A KAYAK	D E L P D A D
2	PRIVATE	E R N I N
3	SPECIFIC CONCERN	H E M E T
4	GRAVITY	P H E D T

MYSTERY ANSWER:

CLUE: Person with a heart for charity.

GOD GIVES FULLNESS OF LIFE

Complete the crossword puzzle by looking at the clues and unscrambling the answers. When the puzzle is complete, unscramble the circled letters to solve the Mystery Answer.

The thief's purpose is to steal and kill and destroy. My purpose is to give them a rich and satisfying life.
JOHN 10:10

ACROSS

1	LOYAL	TUFFHILA
5	COMEBACK	ERNURT
6	POURED DOWN	ADRENI
7	SUFFICIENT	HOUNGE

DOWN

1	WRINKLED	WURFREDO
2	INSIDE	ORINIRTE
3	SUFFERING	GRUNITH
4	ANGRILY	VIDILLY

MYSTERY ANSWER:

CLUE: The Giver of life promises us lives that are _____.

GOD MEETS WITH HIS PEOPLE

Complete the crossword puzzle by looking at the clues and unscrambling the answers. When the puzzle is complete, unscramble the circled letters to solve the Mystery Answer.

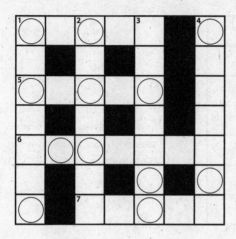

[Jesus said,] "Where two or three gather together as my followers, I am there among them."
MATTHEW 18:20

ACROSS

1	BARBECUE NEEDS	O L A S C
5	SHARE	A R O T I
6	COMMON STRINGS	L O N S I V I
7	AUTOGRAPHS	G N S S I

DOWN

1	DESERT PARADE	N A R C A V A
2	PENS	S T O U R A H
3	DECEIVING	S I G W O N N
4	SAGE HENS	O S S U G E R

MYSTERY ANSWER:

CLUE: Church gathering.

GOD DRIES OUR TEARS

Complete the crossword puzzle by looking at the clues and unscrambling the answers. When the puzzle is complete, unscramble the circled letters to solve the Mystery Answer.

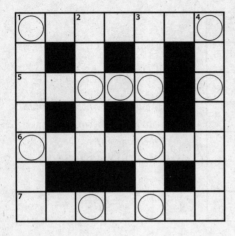

You will weep no more. How gracious he will be when you cry for help! As soon as he hears, he will answer you.

ISAIAH 30:19, NIV

ACROSS

1 MANDARINS   **G E A R O N S**

5 CADENCE   **M E O P T**

6 VIGOROUS   **E S T N I N E**

7 SHEATHED   **D A N C E E S**

DOWN

1 NOT IN THE LOOP   **E O D U S T I**

2 LET PASS   **M A T I D**

3 RESTRICTS   **R U N G D O S**

4 SUSHI WRAP   **E E S E D A W**

MYSTERY ANSWER:

CLUE: **Display of sympathy and understanding.**

GOD RENEWS OUR STRENGTH

Complete the crossword puzzle by looking at the clues and unscrambling the answers. When the puzzle is complete, unscramble the circled letters to solve the Mystery Answer.

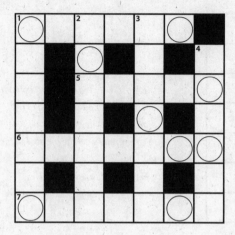

Even youths grow tired and weary, and young men stumble and fall; but those who hope in the LORD will renew their strength. They will soar on wings like eagles; they will run and not grow weary, they will walk and not be faint.

ISAIAH 40:30-31, NIV

ACROSS

1	DIMINISH	CUERDE
5	CACKLE	UGHAL
6	MORE HEATED	RENIGAR
7	SUIT	FISTYAS

DOWN

1	UNCOVERS	VEERLAS
2	ENJOYMENT	THEGLID
3	KINSMEN	SUNCISO
4	PROBLEMATIC	HOTNYR

MYSTERY ANSWER: ☐☐☐☐☐☐☐☐☐☐

CLUE: God _____ your soul.

GOD CHOOSES HIS OWN

Complete the crossword puzzle by looking at the clues and unscrambling the answers. When the puzzle is complete, unscramble the circled letters to solve the Mystery Answer.

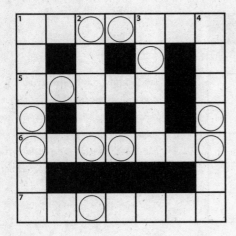

In [Christ] we were also chosen, having been predestined according to the plan of him who works out everything in conformity with the purpose of his will.
EPHESIANS 1:11, NIV

ACROSS

1	COLOR ROLLER	RINPEAT
5	MOUTH TOPS	FOSOR
6	RATHER	TENSIDA
7	PHASED	PEPDEST

DOWN

1	FACTIONS	TIREPAS
2	CHAINS	NISRO
3	SAMPLE	ESATT
4	REMOVED EDGES	DUODNER

MYSTERY ANSWER:

CLUE: **Ultimate end.**

GOD IS OUR ETERNAL GUIDE

Complete the crossword puzzle by looking at the clues and unscrambling the answers. When the puzzle is complete, unscramble the circled letters to solve the Mystery Answer.

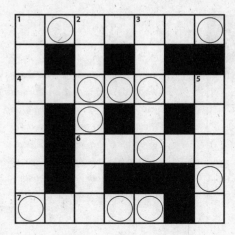

God is our God for ever and ever; he will be our guide even to the end.

PSALM 48:14, NIV

ACROSS

1 DRESSING   **N A G B E D A**

4 MISSIONS   **R O S S I T E**

6 HELD   **W E D O N**

7 FUELS   **A G E S S**

DOWN

1 ENJOYING THE SUN   **G A B N I K S**

2 EDGY   **O R E S N U V**

3 PICK SIDES   **L A I N G**

5 EDGE   **D I L S E**

MYSTERY ANSWER:

CLUE: God's guidance is _____.

GOD IS APPROACHABLE

Complete the crossword puzzle by looking at the clues and unscrambling the answers. When the puzzle is complete, unscramble the circled letters to solve the Mystery Answer.

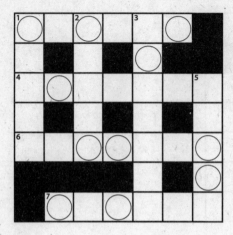

Keep on asking, and you will receive what you ask for. Keep on seeking, and you will find. Keep on knocking, and the door will be opened to you. For everyone who asks, receives. Everyone who seeks, finds. And to everyone who knocks, the door will be opened.

MATTHEW 7:7-8

ACROSS

1	NOT OFTEN	RYERAL
4	INANE	COVAUSU
6	LOATHE	ELIDKIS
7	CRESTS	DESGIR

DOWN

1	RANTED	VADER
2	BROWN AND WILD	CERIS
3	TAKING A PEEK	KILNOGO
5	PERCOLATES	PESSE

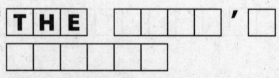

MYSTERY ANSWER: T H E ☐☐☐☐ ' ☐ ☐☐☐☐☐

CLUE: Supplication model.

GOD WILL JUDGE OUR ACTIONS

Complete the crossword puzzle by looking at the clues and unscrambling the answers. When the puzzle is complete, unscramble the circled letters to solve the Mystery Answer.

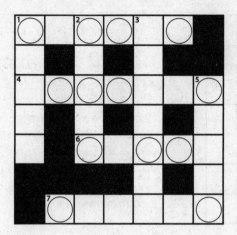

Fear God and obey his commands, for this is everyone's duty. God will judge us for everything we do, including every secret thing, whether good or bad.

ECCLESIASTES 12:13-14

ACROSS

1	POTENTIAL	PISUED
4	DIALING	PINNOGH
6	SPARE	ATREX
7	DIGS UP	PASSED

DOWN

1	SHOE PART	PURPE
2	LONG ROBE	OTELS
3	STRAYED	FEDDIRT
5	NANNIES	GASOT

MYSTERY ANSWER:

CLUE: Product of obedience to God.

GOD PROVIDES VICTORY

Complete the crossword puzzle by looking at the clues and unscrambling the answers. When the puzzle is complete, unscramble the circled letters to solve the Mystery Answer.

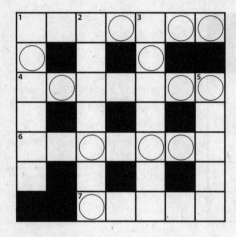

We are hard pressed on every side, but not crushed; perplexed, but not in despair; persecuted, but not abandoned; struck down, but not destroyed. We always carry around in our body the death of Jesus, so that the life of Jesus may also be revealed in our body.

2 CORINTHIANS 4:8-10, NIV

ACROSS

1	ONE WHO BLAMES	C R U S E C A
4	FARM PIECE	C A R T T R O
6	SLANT	L I N N I C E
7	AUDIBLE BREATHS	G I H S S

DOWN

1	REACH	T A N I T A
2	TRIES	S H E N A C C
3	LOCATION	G E S T T I N
5	FLANGED SPOOLS	S L E R E

MYSTERY ANSWER:

CLUE: **Jesus' miraculous victory over death.**

GOD'S LOVE IS UNFAILING

Complete the crossword puzzle by looking at the clues and unscrambling the answers. When the puzzle is complete, unscramble the circled letters to solve the Mystery Answer.

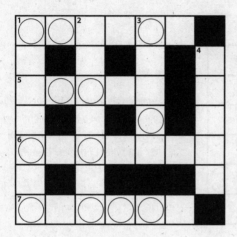

Yahweh! The LORD! The God of compassion and mercy! I am slow to anger and filled with unfailing love and faithfulness.

EXODUS 34:6, NIV

ACROSS

1	ANSWERS	**B U S T E R**
5	POINTS ON A KICK	**H E T E R**
6	RESILIENT	**T E I C A L S**
7	TWO IN LINE	**D A M E N T**

DOWN

1	GETAWAY	**T E R R A T E**
2	DEAL	**G A R I B A N**
3	PAY THE BILL	**R E T T A**
4	TAP	**C A N D E**

MYSTERY ANSWER:

CLUE: Sign of compassion.

GOD WILL COMPLETE OUR GROWTH

Complete the crossword puzzle by looking at the clues and unscrambling the answers. When the puzzle is complete, unscramble the circled letters to solve the Mystery Answer.

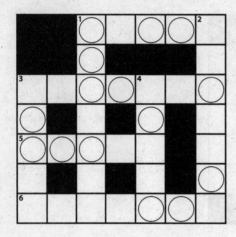

I am certain that God, who began the good work within you, will continue his work until it is finally finished on the day when Christ Jesus returns.

PHILIPPIANS 1:6

ACROSS

1	CRESTS	**A S K E P**
3	SINUOUS	**W O G F I L N**
5	WEDGES AND FIVES	**R I S N O**
6	INNERMOST	**S E P E D E T**

DOWN

1	SUGGEST	**R O P P S O E**
2	WEDGE	**M E S T E N G**
3	OVERHEATED	**R E D I F**
4	EMERGE	**S U S I E**

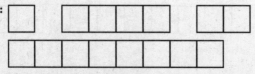

MYSTERY ANSWER:

CLUE: **What we are in Christ.**

144

GOD OFFERS ABUNDANT GRACE

Complete the crossword puzzle by looking at the clues and unscrambling the answers. When the puzzle is complete, unscramble the circled letters to solve the Mystery Answer.

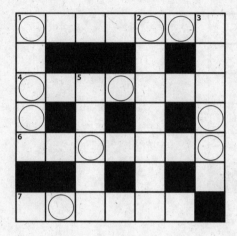

God is able to make all grace abound to you, so that in all things at all times, having all that you need, you will abound in every good work.

2 CORINTHIANS 9:8, NIV

ACROSS

1 MODIFIERS   **DESVABR**

4 TENDER   **IFLUPAN**

6 CAME TO LIGHT   **REEMDEG**

7 ENCOURAGE   **TROFES**

DOWN

1 PIE STAPLE   **ALPEP**

2 ONE WHO FLEES   **GEUEREF**

3 DRESSED GREENS   **DASSLA**

5 ELEMENTS   **TEMSI**

MYSTERY ANSWER:

CLUE: God's grace makes our sins _____.

GOD GIVES SHELTER FROM TROUBLE

Complete the crossword puzzle by looking at the clues and unscrambling the answers. When the puzzle is complete, unscramble the circled letters to solve the Mystery Answer.

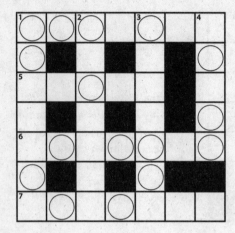

The LORD is good, a strong refuge when trouble comes. He is close to those who trust in him.
NAHUM 1:7

ACROSS

1	EXPOSES	EVERSAL
5	JOCKEY'S COLORS	KILSS
6	SCHOLARLY	NALDEER
7	SCORCHERS	RISSEGN

DOWN

1	FALLOUT	TUSSLER
2	HEAVY	LIVNAIL
3	WANT	BANSCEE
4	INLET	DOSNU

MYSTERY ANSWER:

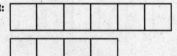

CLUE: **Given to those who trust in the Lord.**

146

GOD WILL PUNISH THE WICKED

Complete the crossword puzzle by looking at the clues and unscrambling the answers. When the puzzle is complete, unscramble the circled letters to solve the Mystery Answer.

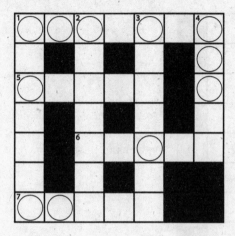

The LORD supports the humble, but he brings the wicked down into the dust.
PSALM 147:6

ACROSS

1	FROM ROME OR PISA	LATAINI
5	OUTSPOKEN	CLOVA
6	DANGLES	NGASH
7	PLAYTHINGS	LOSLD

DOWN

1	OVERRAN	DAVENID
2	RUBBING OR GRAIN	COLLOAH
3	SOLOMON OR CANARY	NALDISS
4	CHIPS	SCINK

MYSTERY ANSWER:

CLUE: Christ's death is our _____.

GOD DISCIPLINES THE ARROGANT

Complete the crossword puzzle by looking at the clues and unscrambling the answers. When the puzzle is complete, unscramble the circled letters to solve the Mystery Answer.

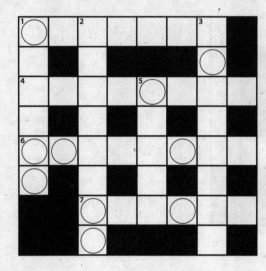

Pride goes before destruction, and haughtiness before a fall.
PROVERBS 16:18

ACROSS

1	ELIMINATE	NUXGEEP
4	HOLD IN CHECK	CHAFFDUN
6	ILLUSTRATION	CASTINNE
7	REPEATS	OSEHEC

DOWN

1	CULTURAL	NIHCET
2	PENALIZED	DINSHUPE
3	ACCOMPLISHED	FEEDCEFT
5	SPAR	ALSCH

MYSTERY ANSWER:

CLUE: Too much of this can be humbling.

148

GOD WILL CREATE A NEW ORDER

Complete the crossword puzzle by looking at the clues and unscrambling the answers. When the puzzle is complete, unscramble the circled letters to solve the Mystery Answer.

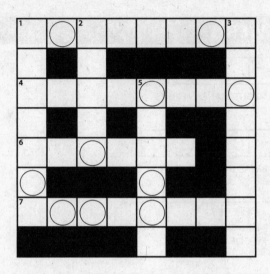

The one sitting on the throne said, "Look, I am making everything new!" And then he said to me, "Write this down, for what I tell you is trustworthy and true."

REVELATION 21:5

ACROSS

1	SKINS	**S L E G P I N E**
4	STRUCK	**K E T T A D A C**
6	FINDING A STATION	**G U N N I T**
7	ROUTINELY	**M Y O N M O L C**

DOWN

1	ARTIFICIAL	**P I L C A T S**
2	INGESTED	**T E A N E**
3	ASKEW	**W I S S A D Y E**
5	ARTILLERY	**N O C N A N**

MYSTERY ANSWER: S ☐☐☐☐☐ C ☐☐☐☐☐

CLUE: Time of Christ's return.

SUPER JUMBLES
GOD'S PEOPLE THRIVE

Unscramble these Jumbles, one letter to each square, to form ordinary words. Then arrange the circled letters to solve the Mystery Answer below.

PUZZLE	ANSWER

#1 VISOLE

CLUE: MEDITERRANEAN FRUITS

#2 GNIRAS

CLUE: BREAD INGREDIENTS

#3 SERVATH

CLUE: TYPE OF MOON

#4 AFRILLNA

CLUE: PRECIPITATION

#5 STAERSPU

CLUE: GRAZING LANDS

#6 ORRYSPITEP

CLUE: SUCCESS

MYSTERY ANSWER:

CLUE: God rewards _____ obedience.

If you carefully obey all the commands I am giving you today, and if you love the Lord your God and serve him with all your heart and soul, then he will send the rains in their proper seasons—the early and late rains—so you can bring in your harvests of grain, new wine, and olive oil. He will give you lush pastureland for your livestock, and you yourselves will have all you want to eat. DEUTERONOMY 11:13-15

150

GOD RESTORES HEALTH

Unscramble these Jumbles, one letter to each square, to form ordinary words. Then arrange the circled letters to solve the Mystery Answer below.

PUZZLE	ANSWER

#1 FIENSTS

⟨◯⟩ ☐ ☐ ☐ ☐ ⟨◯⟩

CLUE: PHYSICAL HEALTH

#2 ROCERVE

☐ ☐ ☐ ⟨◯⟩ ☐ ☐ ☐

CLUE: GET WELL

#3 HEPTRAY

☐ ☐ ☐ ⟨◯⟩ ☐ ☐ ☐

CLUE: TREATMENT

#4 LAYTHEH

☐ ⟨◯⟩ ☐ ☐ ☐ ☐ ☐

CLUE: WELL IN BODY

#5 YILIVATT

☐ ☐ ☐ ☐ ⟨◯⟩ ☐ ☐ ☐

CLUE: POWER TO GROW

#6 GLENIBLEW

⟨◯⟩ ☐ ☐ ☐ - ☐ ☐ ☐ ☐ ☐

CLUE: HEALTH AND HAPPINESS

MYSTERY ANSWER: ☐ ☐ ☐ ☐ ☐ ☐ ☐ ☐

CLUE: A gift for someone who is under the weather.

"I will give you back your health and heal your wounds," says the Lord. JEREMIAH 30:17

GOD DEVELOPS OUR CHARACTER

Unscramble these Jumbles, one letter to each square, to form ordinary words. Then arrange the circled letters to solve the Mystery Answer below.

PUZZLE	ANSWER

#1 FUNFESSILATH

☐☐☐☐☐☐◯☐☐☐☐☐

CLUE: LOYALTY

#2 OILGVN

◯☐☐☐☐☐

CLUE: AFFECTIONATE

#3 LOJYUF

◯☐☐☐☐☐

CLUE: CAREFREE

#4 CENITPEA

☐☐☐☐☐◯☐☐

CLUE: FORTITUDE

#5 ECALPFUE

☐☐☐☐◯☐☐☐

CLUE: CALM

#6 SOGESNOD

◯☐☐☐☐☐☐☐

CLUE: INTEGRITY

MYSTERY ANSWER: ☐☐☐☐☐☐

CLUE: **An abundance of branches and fruit is found here.**

He cuts off every branch of mine that doesn't produce fruit, and he prunes the branches that do bear fruit so they will produce even more. JOHN 15:2

GOD EMBRACES HIS FAMILY

Unscramble these Jumbles, one letter to each square, to form ordinary words. Then arrange the circled letters to solve the Mystery Answer below.

PUZZLE	ANSWER

#1 DOBOR

CLUE: HATCHLINGS

#2 IFLMAY

CLUE: RELATIVES

#3 EGIARTHE

CLUE: ETHNIC BACKGROUND

#4 GANEILE

CLUE: FAMILY TREE

#5 SHOEDULHO

CLUE: FAMILY CIRCLE

#6 FONGSPRIF

CLUE: DESCENDANT

MYSTERY ANSWER:

CLUE: In God's family, we _____ .

No, I will not abandon you as orphans—I will come to you. JOHN 14:18

GOD GRANTS SAFETY

Unscramble these Jumbles, one letter to each square, to form ordinary words. Then arrange the circled letters to solve the Mystery Answer below.

PUZZLE	ANSWER

#1 S I O S A

☐ Ⓞ ☐ ☐ ☐

CLUE: WATERING HOLE

#2 V A N E H

Ⓞ ☐ ☐ ☐ ☐

CLUE: SAFE PLACE

#3 F U R E E G

☐ ☐ Ⓞ ☐ ☐ ☐

CLUE: ASYLUM

#4 B A R R O H

☐ ☐ ☐ ☐ Ⓞ ☐

CLUE: CONCEAL

#5 E T H E R L S

☐ ☐ ☐ ☐ Ⓞ ☐ ☐

CLUE: COVER

#6 R A T T E E R

☐ ☐ ☐ ☐ ☐ Ⓞ ☐

CLUE: HIDEAWAY

MYSTERY ANSWER: ☐ ☐ ☐ ☐ ☐ ☐

CLUE: Because God is your _____, he will keep you safe.

Taste and see that the LORD is good. Oh, the joys of those who take refuge in him! PSALM 34:8

GOD FORGIVES SINS

Unscramble these Jumbles, one letter to each square, to form ordinary words. Then arrange the circled letters to solve the Mystery Answer below.

PUZZLE	ANSWER

#1 LAWFLONS

CLUE: SKIER'S DELIGHT

#2 ROIVY

CLUE: PIANO KEY

#3 WOLGIGN

CLUE: RADIANT

#4 POLSTSES

CLUE: WITHOUT BLEMISH

#5 NAGGLENI

CLUE: FOLLOWING THE REAPER

#6 NOCTNINE

CLUE: JURY VERDICT

MYSTERY ANSWER:

CLUE: God can forgive your sins and make you as white as a _____ sheep.

"Come now, let's settle this," says the Lord. "Though your sins are like scarlet, I will make them as white as snow. Though they are red like crimson, I will make them as white as wool." ISAIAH 1:18

GOD HEALS

Unscramble these Jumbles, one letter to each square, to form ordinary words. Then arrange the circled letters to solve the Mystery Answer below.

PUZZLE	ANSWER

#1 ICTNO

⬜⬜⬜🔘⬜

CLUE: REFRESHER

#2 COTORD

⬜⬜⬜⬜⬜🔘

CLUE: MODIFY

#3 PREERIAD

🔘⬜⬜⬜⬜⬜⬜⬜

CLUE: FIXED

#4 PYTHAC

🔘⬜⬜⬜⬜🔘

CLUE: UNEVEN

#5 GABNADE

⬜🔘⬜⬜⬜⬜⬜

CLUE: BIND A WOUND

#6 DIECENIM

🔘⬜⬜⬜⬜⬜⬜⬜

CLUE: ASPIRIN

MYSTERY ANSWER: ⬜⬜⬜⬜⬜⬜⬜

CLUE: God is our _____ physician.

By his wounds you are healed. 1 PETER 2:24

GOD COMFORTS

Unscramble these Jumbles, one letter to each square, to form ordinary words. Then arrange the circled letters to solve the Mystery Answer below.

PUZZLE	ANSWER

#1 ERECH

⬜⬜⬜⬜⬜ (circles: 1, 4)

CLUE: "GO, FIGHT, WIN!"

#2 HOESTO

⬜⬜⬜⬜⬜⬜ (circle: 6)

CLUE: TREAT WITH ALOE

#3 SELOCA

⬜⬜⬜⬜⬜⬜ (circle: 4)

CLUE: RELIEF

#4 HEDFRESER

⬜⬜⬜⬜⬜⬜⬜⬜⬜ (circles: 1, 3)

CLUE: INVIGORATED

#5 LEDDANG

⬜⬜⬜⬜⬜⬜⬜ (circles: 1, 3)

CLUE: HEARTEN

#6 LOOCANNOTIS

⬜⬜⬜⬜⬜⬜⬜⬜⬜⬜⬜ (circle: 3)

CLUE: COMFORT

MYSTERY ANSWER:

⬜⬜⬜⬜⬜⬜⬜⬜⬜⬜

CLUE: **A comforting aroma.**

He comforts us in all our troubles so that we can comfort others. When they are troubled, we will be able to give them the same comfort God has given us. 2 CORINTHIANS 1:4

GOD DEFENDS

Unscramble these Jumbles, one letter to each square, to form ordinary words. Then arrange the circled letters to solve the Mystery Answer below.

PUZZLE	ANSWER

#1 GLUSTGER

CLUE: GRAPPLE

#2 ARAUDING

CLUE: PROTECTOR

#3 FREDDENE

CLUE: BACKER

#4 COINPETTOR

CLUE: SHIELD

#5 MAHACINIL

CLUE: KNIGHT'S ARMOR

#6 TEVADOAC

CLUE: PLEAD FOR

MYSTERY ANSWER:

CLUE: As our _____, God goes before us into battle.

The LORD himself will fight for you. Just stay calm. EXODUS 14:14

GOD ANSWERS PRAYERS

Unscramble these Jumbles, one letter to each square, to form ordinary words. Then arrange the circled letters to solve the Mystery Answer below.

PUZZLE	ANSWER

#1 TRADGEN

CLUE: ALLOWED

#2 FROCNIM

CLUE: VERIFY

#3 DIVORPE

CLUE: SUPPLY

#4 LIFLLUF

CLUE: PERFORM

#5 YASFIST

CLUE: SUIT

#6 DERPENDOS

CLUE: REPLIED

MYSTERY ANSWER:

CLUE: How God responds to our requests.

We are confident that he hears us whenever we ask for anything that pleases him. And since we know he hears us when we make our requests, we also know that he will give us what we ask for. 1 JOHN 5:14-15

159

GOD IS OUR ADVOCATE

Unscramble these Jumbles, one letter to each square, to form ordinary words. Then arrange the circled letters to solve the Mystery Answer below.

PUZZLE	ANSWER

#1 IRVOFEAT

CLUE: BELOVED

#2 NEFEDD

CLUE: UPHOLD

#3 TRUPOSP

CLUE: BUTTRESS

#4 TRECOORPT

CLUE: GUARDIAN

#5 NOSUECL

CLUE: GUIDANCE

#6 PEMTOOR

CLUE: ADVANCE

MYSTERY ANSWER:

CLUE: One who advocates.

My dear children, I am writing this to you so that you will not sin. But if anyone does sin, we have an advocate who pleads our case before the Father. He is Jesus Christ, the one who is truly righteous. **1 JOHN 2:1**

GOD SACRIFICED FOR US

Unscramble these Jumbles, one letter to each square, to form ordinary words. Then arrange the circled letters to solve the Mystery Answer below.

PUZZLE	ANSWER

#1 GILIDENY

CLUE: COMPLIANT

#2 VEDETO

CLUE: COMMIT

#3 MORRDTAMY

CLUE: SACRIFICIAL DEATH

#4 EFITROF

CLUE: GIVE UP

#5 DUNEDRE

CLUE: PUT UP WITH

#6 GOFIFREN

CLUE: TITHE

MYSTERY ANSWER:

CLUE: Christ _____ the verdict we deserve.

We know what real love is because Jesus gave up his life for us. 1 JOHN 3:16

GOD BLESSES HIS CHILDREN

Unscramble these Jumbles, one letter to each square, to form ordinary words. Then arrange the circled letters to solve the Mystery Answer below.

PUZZLE	ANSWER

#1 S P O R C

⬜⬜⬜⬜⬜

CLUE: A FARMER'S HOPE

#2 R I F F U T L Y

⬜⬜⬜⬜⬜⬜   ⬜⬜⬜

CLUE: ORCHARD PEST

#3 L E G G I A N N

⬜⬜⬜⬜⬜⬜⬜⬜

CLUE: GARNERING

#4 U N A M U T

⬜⬜⬜⬜⬜⬜

CLUE: PUMPKIN TIME

#5 T H I N G G R E A

⬜⬜⬜⬜⬜⬜⬜⬜⬜

CLUE: COLLECTION

#6 T A R R V E E S H

⬜⬜⬜⬜⬜⬜⬜⬜

CLUE: COMBINE

MYSTERY ANSWER:

⬜⬜⬜⬜⬜⬜⬜

CLUE: Garden green.

Let's not get tired of doing what is good. At just the right time we will reap a harvest of blessing if we don't give up. Therefore, whenever we have the opportunity, we should do good to everyone—especially to those in the family of faith. GALATIANS 6:9-10

GOD GIVES INSIGHT

Unscramble these Jumbles, one letter to each square, to form ordinary words. Then arrange the circled letters to solve the Mystery Answer below.

PUZZLE	ANSWER

#1 ANELRING

CLUE: STUDENT'S JOB

#2 IMDOWS

CLUE: SOLOMON'S GIFT

#3 IVYNOSIRA

CLUE: PROPHET

#4 GINSITH

CLUE: INTUITION

#5 CHASSLOR

CLUE: STUDENTS

#6 TIDAMICENSIR

CLUE: SINGLE OUT

MYSTERY ANSWER:

CLUE: Unnecessary tool for communicating with God.

Call to me and I will answer you and tell you great and unsearchable things you do not know.
JEREMIAH 33:3, NIV

163

GOD EXTENDS COMPASSION

Unscramble these Jumbles, one letter to each square, to form ordinary words. Then arrange the circled letters to solve the Mystery Answer below.

PUZZLE	ANSWER

#1 FRIMECUL

CLUE: FORGIVING

#2 OSUCARIG

CLUE: BENEVOLENT

#3 MARWHT

CLUE: AFFECTION

#4 ERSOMER

CLUE: DEEP REGRET

#5 THYCIAR

CLUE: GOODWILL

#6 MAYTHYPS

CLUE: PITY

MYSTERY ANSWER:

CLUE: Joseph's younger son.

I remember my affliction and my wandering, the bitterness and the gall. I well remember them, and my soul is downcast within me. Yet this I call to mind and therefore I have hope: Because of the LORD's great love we are not consumed, for his compassions never fail. LAMENTATIONS 3:19-22, NIV

GOD PROVIDES FREEDOM

Unscramble these Jumbles, one letter to each square, to form ordinary words. Then arrange the circled letters to solve the Mystery Answer below.

PUZZLE	ANSWER

#1 ITREBLY

CLUE: FREEDOM

#2 ELEURIS

CLUE: FREE TIME

#3 AESRELE

CLUE: LET GO

#4 YUMIMINT

CLUE: EXEMPTION

#5 IVPIERGEL

CLUE: LICENSE

#6 MYNOOTUA

CLUE: SELF-RULE

MYSTERY ANSWER:

CLUE: Length of our freedom with Christ.

In my distress I prayed to the LORD, and the LORD answered me and set me free. PSALM 118:5

GOD IS OUR ROCK

Unscramble these Jumbles, one letter to each square, to form ordinary words. Then arrange the circled letters to solve the Mystery Answer below.

PUZZLE	ANSWER

#1 GUFREE

CLUE: SHELTER

#2 DELDESIH

CLUE: PROTECTED

#3 CREFORMOT

CLUE: CONSOLER

#4 TRYSUECI

CLUE: SAFETY

#5 GRIVINLEE

CLUE: ALLAYING

#6 CRINTOOPET

CLUE: DEFENSE

MYSTERY ANSWER:

CLUE: **These first responders keep you safe.**

[David] sang: "The LORD is my rock, my fortress, and my savior; my God is my rock, in whom I find protection. He is my shield, the power that saves me, and my place of safety. He is my refuge, my savior, the one who saves me from violence." 2 SAMUEL 22:2-3

GOD PROVIDES STRENGTH

Unscramble these Jumbles, one letter to each square, to form ordinary words. Then arrange the circled letters to solve the Mystery Answer below.

PUZZLE	ANSWER

#1 HITRYOUTA

CLUE: CLOUT

#2 WOLFPURE

CLUE: INFLUENTIAL

#3 SIGROOVU

CLUE: FORCEFUL

#4 SMULEC

CLUE: BRAWN

#5 GREENZIES

CLUE: BOOSTS

#6 MUTOMMNE

CLUE: THRUST

MYSTERY ANSWER:

CLUE: **Exceeds in importance.**

My health may fail, and my spirit may grow weak, but God remains the strength of my heart; he is mine forever.

PSALM 73:26

167

GOD SENDS GUARDIAN ANGELS

Unscramble these Jumbles, one letter to each square, to form ordinary words. Then arrange the circled letters to solve the Mystery Answer below.

PUZZLE	ANSWER

#1 C H A W T R E

CLUE: OBSERVER

#2 S E F N E D D

CLUE: SECURES

#3 P U R B E S M

CLUE: CUSHIONS

#4 S C I E N T R O G

CLUE: ATTENDING

#5 C R O W W A T T E H

CLUE: SENTRY'S PERCH

#6 R A L G P I N T O L

CLUE: WALKING THE BEAT

MYSTERY ANSWER:

CLUE: Angels in God's army.

[The Most High] will command his angels concerning you to guard you in all your ways. **PSALM 91:11, NIV**

GOD MAKES US NEW CREATIONS

Unscramble these Jumbles, one letter to each square, to form ordinary words. Then arrange the circled letters to solve the Mystery Answer below.

PUZZLE	ANSWER

#1 NEGERTEERA

CLUE: REVIVE

#2 LUNTARA

CLUE: INBORN

#3 WEERNLA

CLUE: REBIRTH

#4 SHEFERR

CLUE: INVIGORATE

#5 ANGLIRIO

CLUE: FIRST DRAFT

#6 ROTREES

CLUE: RENEW

MYSTERY ANSWER:

CLUE: When God forgives sins, they are also _____.

Anyone who belongs to Christ has become a new person. The old life is gone; a new life has begun!
2 CORINTHIANS 5:17

GOD EXTENDS HIS HOLINESS

Unscramble these Jumbles, one letter to each square, to form ordinary words. Then arrange the circled letters to solve the Mystery Answer below.

PUZZLE	ANSWER

#1 DECETEL

CLUE: CHOSEN

#2 DASSENERCS

CLUE: HOLINESS

#3 HOECIC

CLUE: DECISION

#4 TRAVENEED

CLUE: BLESSED

#5 DOVDETE

CLUE: COMMITTED

#6 VEERNTER

CLUE: AWED

MYSTERY ANSWER:

CLUE: God's people are _____ with him.

*You are a holy people, who belong to the L*ORD *your God. Of all the people on earth, the L*ORD *your God has chosen you to be his own special treasure.* DEUTERONOMY 7:6

GOD GIVES PERSEVERANCE

Unscramble these Jumbles, one letter to each square, to form ordinary words. Then arrange the circled letters to solve the Mystery Answer below.

PUZZLE	ANSWER

#1 STAIDYVER

CLUE: DIFFICULTY

#2 ATNAMIS

CLUE: FORTITUDE

#3 SPEERISCENT

CLUE: DILIGENCE

#4 TANCEPEI

CLUE: TOLERANCE

#5 OSCENITAU

CLUE: DRIVEN

#6 GESDODSENG

CLUE: RESOLVE

MYSTERY ANSWER:

CLUE: Given by Christ to each of his followers.

Dear brothers and sisters, when troubles come your way, consider it an opportunity for great joy. For you know that when your faith is tested, your endurance has a chance to grow. So let it grow, for when your endurance is fully developed, you will be perfect and complete, needing nothing. JAMES 1:2-4

GOD RESTORES HIS PEOPLE

Unscramble these Jumbles, one letter to each square, to form ordinary words. Then arrange the circled letters to solve the Mystery Answer below.

PUZZLE	ANSWER

#1 WATTLARS

CLUE: UNWAVERING

#2 GUYNNELIDI

CLUE: FIRM

#3 DELIRMEAC

CLUE: SALVAGED

#4 DESTAISE

CLUE: MAKES FIRM

#5 CYLSEUER

CLUE: FIRMLY

#6 IBENGLUDIR

CLUE: RENOVATION

MYSTERY ANSWER:

CLUE: Doctor's fix-it.

In his kindness God called you to share in his eternal glory by means of Christ Jesus. So after you have suffered a little while, he will restore, support, and strengthen you, and he will place you on a firm foundation.
1 PETER 5:10

GOD IS ACCESSIBLE

Unscramble these Jumbles, one letter to each square, to form ordinary words. Then arrange the circled letters to solve the Mystery Answer below.

PUZZLE	ANSWER

#1 CLORIDA

CLUE: AMIABLE

#2 WUFORSROL

CLUE: SADDENED

#3 PYHAMET

CLUE: COMPASSION

#4 MAIZEROHN

CLUE: CORRESPOND

#5 TIFAYFIN

CLUE: KINSHIP

#6 SIKSENND

CLUE: SYMPATHY

MYSTERY ANSWER:

CLUE: Jesus becomes our _____ to God.

We do not have a high priest who is unable to sympathize with our weaknesses, but we have one who has been tempted in every way, just as we are—yet was without sin. Let us then approach the throne of grace with confidence, so that we may receive mercy and find grace to help us in our time of need. **HEBREWS 4:15-16, NIV**

GOD MEETS NEEDS

Unscramble these Jumbles, one letter to each square, to form ordinary words. Then arrange the circled letters to solve the Mystery Answer below.

PUZZLE	ANSWER

#1 PILSCEED

CLUE: HID

#2 DWEENOD

CLUE: FUNDED

#3 DEENDERR

CLUE: MADE

#4 TEADIFISS

CLUE: CONTENT

#5 ONSHIRU

CLUE: FOSTER

#6 RESINPHEL

CLUE: STOCK UP

MYSTERY ANSWER:

CLUE: God's role with our needs.

This same God who takes care of me will supply all your needs from his glorious riches, which have been given to us in Christ Jesus. PHILIPPIANS 4:19

GOD GIVES PURPOSE

Unscramble these Jumbles, one letter to each square, to form ordinary words. Then arrange the circled letters to solve the Mystery Answer below.

PUZZLE	ANSWER

#1 EDGENIDS

CLUE: DELIBERATE

#2 OTINNETNI

CLUE: OBJECTIVE

#3 AESSNOR

CLUE: BASES

#4 SIOMNIS

CLUE: DUTY

#5 CUFNINTO

CLUE: GO

#6 BINITOMA

CLUE: AIM

MYSTERY ANSWER:

CLUE: The Lord's plans and _____ are always perfect.

You can make many plans, but the Lord's purpose will prevail. PROVERBS 19:21

GOD STRENGTHENS WITH COURAGE

Unscramble these Jumbles, one letter to each square, to form ordinary words. Then arrange the circled letters to solve the Mystery Answer below.

PUZZLE	ANSWER

#1 DRIPINET

CLUE: VALIANT

#2 DARVOBA

CLUE: DARING

#3 LATLANG

CLUE: VALIANT

#4 USOGAROCUE

CLUE: DARING

#5 ERASFELS

CLUE: VALIANT

#6 DRENATUVUSO

CLUE: DARING

MYSTERY ANSWER:

CLUE: By-product of courage.

Be strong and courageous! Do not be afraid and do not panic before them. For the LORD your God will personally go ahead of you. He will neither fail you nor abandon you. DEUTERONOMY 31:6

GOD KEEPS HIS PROMISES

Unscramble these Jumbles, one letter to each square, to form ordinary words. Then arrange the circled letters to solve the Mystery Answer below.

PUZZLE	ANSWER

#1 BISOLISTYIP

☐☐☐☐☐☐☐☐Ⓞ☐

CLUE: PROSPECT

#2 TENLOTIPA

☐☐☐Ⓞ☐☐☐☐☐

CLUE: PROSPECTIVE

#3 CASARUNES

Ⓞ☐☐Ⓞ☐☐☐☐

CLUE: PLEDGE

#4 SOPEMIRD

☐☐☐Ⓞ☐☐☐☐

CLUE: VOWED

#5 ANEATRUGE

Ⓞ☐☐☐Ⓞ☐Ⓞ☐

CLUE: ENSURE

#6 TICMOTEMD

☐☐☐☐☐☐Ⓞ☐☐

CLUE: FAITHFUL

MYSTERY ANSWER: ☐☐☐☐☐☐☐☐☐

CLUE: To follow God is to be in _____ with his will.

Understand, therefore, that the LORD your God is indeed God. He is the faithful God who keeps his covenant for a thousand generations and lavishes his unfailing love on those who love him and obey his commands.

DEUTERONOMY 7:9

GOD GIVES PROSPERITY

Unscramble these Jumbles, one letter to each square, to form ordinary words. Then arrange the circled letters to solve the Mystery Answer below.

PUZZLE	ANSWER

#1 SHREVIT

CLUE: PROSPERS

#2 GROBNEUS

CLUE: BLOOMS

#3 SCUECEDS

CLUE: DOES WELL

#4 FRISLOHU

CLUE: FANFARE

#5 SPERGORS

CLUE: MOVEMENT

#6 NUTDANBA

CLUE: RICH

MYSTERY ANSWER:

CLUE: God supplies your daily _____.

Trust in the LORD and do good. Then you will live safely in the land and prosper. **PSALM 37:3**

TRIVIA JUMBLES
GOD SUSTAINS US

Unscramble these Jumbles, one letter to each square, to form ordinary words. Then arrange the circled letters to solve the Mystery Answer below.

PUZZLE	ANSWER

#1 UHRGYN

#2 TIRNSGUT

#3 LYNPET

#4 SHYRITT

#5 OIPNIROVS

#6 CANNEADUB

MYSTERY ANSWER:

CLUE: Essential for physical well-being.

TRIVIA: How much water does a human being need to consume daily?

Even strong young lions sometimes go hungry, but those who trust in the LORD will lack no good thing.

PSALM 34:10

179

GOD ABOUNDS IN LOVE

Unscramble these Jumbles, one letter to each square, to form ordinary words. Then arrange the circled letters to solve the Mystery Answer below.

PUZZLE	ANSWER
#1 GLEENT	☐ ◯ ☐ ◯ ☐ ☐
#2 SEAPINTT	☐ ☐ ◯ ☐ ☐ ◯
#3 THIUFFLA	☐ ◯ ☐ ☐ ☐ ☐
#4 CERMULIF	☐ ◯ ☐ ☐ ☐ ◯
#5 GUSCORIA	☐ ☐ ☐ ◯ ☐ ◯
#6 DUNPROOF	☐ ◯ ☐ ☐ ☐ ☐

MYSTERY ANSWER: ☐ ☐ ☐ ☐ ☐ ☐ ☐ ☐ ☐ ☐ ☐

CLUE: People who received God's love and compassion.

TRIVIA: What is the only country in the world that revolves around the Hebrew calendar?

You, O Lord, are a God of compassion and mercy, slow to get angry and filled with unfailing love and faithfulness. PSALM 86:15

GOD PROVIDES TEACHERS

Unscramble these Jumbles, one letter to each square, to form ordinary words. Then arrange the circled letters to solve the Mystery Answer below.

PUZZLE	ANSWER
#1 PULFDREI	☐ Ⓞ ☐ ☐ ☐ ☐ ☐ ☐
#2 SEERLD	Ⓞ ☐ ☐ ☐ ☐ ☐
#3 BISTUM	☐ ☐ ☐ ☐ ☐ Ⓞ
#4 TOMEDYS	☐ Ⓞ ☐ ☐ ☐ ☐ ☐
#5 TUMLYHII	☐ ☐ Ⓞ ☐ ☐ ☐ ☐ ☐
#6 MENSEKES	☐ ☐ ☐ ☐ Ⓞ ☐ ☐ ☐

MYSTERY ANSWER: ☐ ☐ ☐ ☐ ☐ ☐ ☐

CLUE: The older generation can _____ the younger one.

TRIVIA: Samuel was a great Hebrew prophet. What was the name of the priest who taught him?

You younger men must accept the authority of the elders. And all of you, serve each other in humility, for "God opposes the proud but favors the humble." 1 PETER 5:5

GOD OFFERS PERFECT PEACE

Unscramble these Jumbles, one letter to each square, to form ordinary words. Then arrange the circled letters to solve the Mystery Answer below.

PUZZLE	ANSWER

#1 FLILONGE ☐◯☐☐☐☐☐☐

#2 ERELANT ◯☐☐◯☐☐☐

#3 OVERREF ☐◯☐☐☐☐☐

#4 DUNFILM ◯☐☐☐☐☐☐

#5 TRAPMENEN ◯☐☐☐☐☐☐☐☐

#6 FESTDASTA ◯☐☐☐☐☐◯☐☐

MYSTERY ANSWER: ☐☐☐☐☐☐☐☐☐

CLUE: Trusting God's _____ brings peace.

TRIVIA: What is the Hebrew greeting meaning peace?

You will keep in perfect peace all who trust in you, all whose thoughts are fixed on you! Trust in the LORD always, for the LORD GOD is the eternal Rock. ISAIAH 26:3-4

GOD GIVES HEAVENLY REWARD

Unscramble these Jumbles, one letter to each square, to form ordinary words. Then arrange the circled letters to solve the Mystery Answer below.

PUZZLE	ANSWER

#1 ICYCURF

#2 FURFES

#3 CVMITI

#4 NERMOTT

#5 ROTTEUR

#6 SEPRETCUE

MYSTERY ANSWER:

CLUE: Present suffering can lead to _____ blessing.

TRIVIA: Which disciple was crucified upside down?

God blesses those who are persecuted for doing right, for the Kingdom of Heaven is theirs. MATTHEW 5:10

GOD SECURES VICTORY

Unscramble these Jumbles, one letter to each square, to form ordinary words. Then arrange the circled letters to solve the Mystery Answer below.

PUZZLE	ANSWER
#1 USILGOOR	☐☐☐Ⓞ☐☐☐☐
#2 PRUHTIM	☐☐☐Ⓞ☐Ⓞ☐
#3 IVRYTOC	☐Ⓞ☐☐☐☐☐
#4 QEUNORC	☐Ⓞ☐☐☐Ⓞ
#5 DECSCEU	Ⓞ☐☐☐☐☐☐
#6 MEROCEVO	☐☐Ⓞ☐☐☐☐☐

MYSTERY ANSWER: ☐☐☐☐☐☐☐☐☐☐

CLUE: With God's help, our strength is _____ to our enemies'.

TRIVIA: What was the name of young David's supersized enemy?

Yes, the LORD is for me; he will help me. I will look in triumph at those who hate me. PSALM 118:7

GOD GRANTS DREAMS

Unscramble these Jumbles, one letter to each square, to form ordinary words. Then arrange the circled letters to solve the Mystery Answer below.

PUZZLE	ANSWER

#1 NYSAIVIOR

#2 HISEWS

#3 NILGONG

#4 NIPSOSA

#5 DANRIMGE

#6 IRNNGAYE

MYSTERY ANSWER:

CLUE: God's gifts are greater than we can _____.

TRIVIA: An old man named Simeon met Mary and Joseph at the Temple. What desire did God grant for Simeon?

Delight yourself in the LORD and he will give you the desires of your heart. PSALM 37:4, NIV

GOD PROVIDES HEAVENLY RICHES

Unscramble these Jumbles, one letter to each square, to form ordinary words. Then arrange the circled letters to solve the Mystery Answer below.

PUZZLE	ANSWER

#1 LAWTIERHE

#2 HISRECT

#3 NERDHIITE

#4 PATACIL

#5 NOUFRET

#6 BOSTUNIE

MYSTERY ANSWER:

CLUE: Earthly treasures are _____.

TRIVIA: Who was the wealthiest monarch in the Bible?

Don't be dismayed when the wicked grow rich and their homes become ever more splendid. For when they die, they take nothing with them. Their wealth will not follow them into the grave. PSALM 49:16-17

GOD MENDS HEARTS

Unscramble these Jumbles, one letter to each square, to form ordinary words. Then arrange the circled letters to solve the Mystery Answer below.

PUZZLE	ANSWER
#1 TEACHAT	☐☐☐☐◯◯☐
#2 ETRAPERE	☐☐◯☐☐☐☐☐
#3 BURLIET	☐☐☐◯☐☐☐
#4 MIVPREO	☐☐☐☐☐☐◯
#5 TERSERO	◯☐◯☐☐☐☐
#6 VITALEALE	☐☐☐◯☐☐☐☐☐

MYSTERY ANSWER: ☐☐☐☐☐☐☐ ☐☐

CLUE: God _____ _____ the downcast.

TRIVIA: The Bible's shortest verse is "Jesus wept" (John 11:35, NIV). What was the occasion that brought Christ's tears?

He heals the brokenhearted and bandages their wounds. PSALM 147:3

GOD GRANTS PEACE

Unscramble these Jumbles, one letter to each square, to form ordinary words. Then arrange the circled letters to solve the Mystery Answer below.

PUZZLE	ANSWER
#1 PADCIL	☐☐☐☐⊚
#2 ERLENESY	☐☐☐⊚☐☐☐
#3 DREXEAL	☐☐⊚☐☐☐
#4 DECENTNOT	⊚☐☐☐☐☐☐☐
#5 CASSMELN	☐☐☐⊚☐⊚
#6 LUNYRITALQ	☐☐⊚☐☐☐☐☐☐

MYSTERY ANSWER: ☐☐☐☐☐☐☐☐

CLUE: Like _____ in the darkness is God's peace on earth.

TRIVIA: What Bible characters coined the phrase "Peace on earth"?

Peace I leave with you; my peace I give you. I do not give to you as the world gives. Do not let your hearts be troubled and do not be afraid. JOHN 14:27, NIV

GOD BEARS OUR BURDENS

Unscramble these Jumbles, one letter to each square, to form ordinary words. Then arrange the circled letters to solve the Mystery Answer below.

PUZZLE	ANSWER

#1 VESHAINES ▢▢◯▢◯▢▢▢▢

#2 LASCOOLS ▢▢◯▢◯▢▢▢

#3 DEBRUNED ▢▢◯▢▢▢▢▢

#4 DOULBERT ◯▢▢◯▢▢▢▢

#5 WUNYLIDE ◯▢▢▢▢▢◯▢

#6 BOMCUSMEER ◯▢◯▢▢▢▢▢▢▢

MYSTERY ANSWER: ▢▢▢▢▢▢▢▢▢▢▢▢▢▢

CLUE: **Strength to carry heavy loads.**

TRIVIA: How many muscle categories are in the human body?

Praise the Lord; praise God our savior! For each day he carries us in his arms. PSALM 68:19

GOD IS COMMITTED TO YOU

Unscramble these Jumbles, one letter to each square, to form ordinary words. Then arrange the circled letters to solve the Mystery Answer below.

PUZZLE	ANSWER

#1 GLESDEP ☐☐☐☐◯☐☐

#2 ATRYET ☐◯☐◯☐☐

#3 VACTENNO ☐☐☐☐◯☐☐

#4 VODOEINT ☐☐☐☐◯☐☐

#5 TANCTORC ☐☐☐◯☐☐☐

#6 ETANEMERG ☐☐◯☐◯☐☐☐

MYSTERY ANSWER: ☐☐☐☐☐☐☐☐☐

CLUE: **Covenant between a bride and groom.**

TRIVIA: An object or sign often accompanied ancient covenants and became a visual reminder of the commitment. God gave Noah and the world the rainbow as a sign that he would never again destroy the world by flood.

"The mountains may move and the hills disappear, but even then my faithful love for you will remain. My covenant of blessing will never be broken," says the LORD, who has mercy on you. ISAIAH 54:10

GOD CARES FOR CREATION

Unscramble these Jumbles, one letter to each square, to form ordinary words. Then arrange the circled letters to solve the Mystery Answer below.

PUZZLE	ANSWER

#1 GROYWIRN

#2 EREGNER

#3 DOHLBE

#4 TEANTANDT

#5 CORNNEC

#6 SERENTTI

MYSTERY ANSWER:

CLUE: The _____ provides us with sweetness.

TRIVIA: There are more than 200,000 species of flowers on earth.

If God cares so wonderfully for flowers that are here today and thrown into the fire tomorrow, he will certainly care for you. Why do you have so little faith? LUKE 12:28

GOD PARTNERS WITH US

Unscramble these Jumbles, one letter to each square, to form ordinary words. Then arrange the circled letters to solve the Mystery Answer below.

PUZZLE	ANSWER
#1 YELLSOC	⬚⬚⬚⬚⬚⬚⬚
#2 DATMEN	⬚⬚⬚⬚⬚
#3 ABREYN	⬚⬚⬚⬚⬚
#4 EIBSED	⬚⬚⬚⬚⬚
#5 JONDIA	⬚⬚⬚⬚⬚
#6 CYONAMPAC	⬚⬚⬚⬚⬚⬚⬚⬚

MYSTERY ANSWER: ⬚⬚⬚⬚⬚⬚⬚⬚⬚⬚

CLUE: Jesus is our truest _____.

TRIVIA: When enemies persecuted God's prophet Elisha, God sent horses and chariots of fire to surround and protect him. Read the story in 2 Kings 6.

Do not be afraid or discouraged, for the LORD will personally go ahead of you. He will be with you; he will neither fail you nor abandon you. DEUTERONOMY 31:8

192

GOD GIVES REST

Unscramble these Jumbles, one letter to each square, to form ordinary words. Then arrange the circled letters to solve the Mystery Answer below.

PUZZLE	ANSWER
#1 CANPAT	☐☐☐☐◯☐
#2 ENISTYRE	◯☐☐◯☐☐☐☐
#3 EDUQTEI	☐☐☐◯☐☐☐
#4 QINRULAT	☐☐☐☐☐◯☐☐
#5 NILSSLEST	☐☐☐☐◯☐☐☐☐
#6 XITREALNOA	◯☐☐◯☐☐☐☐☐☐

MYSTERY ANSWER: ☐☐☐☐☐☐☐☐☐

CLUE: Resting in the Lord brings _____.

TRIVIA: A standard cattle yoke weighs 150 pounds.

Jesus said, "Come to me, all of you who are weary and carry heavy burdens, and I will give you rest. Take my yoke upon you. Let me teach you, because I am humble and gentle at heart, and you will find rest for your souls. For my yoke is easy to bear, and the burden I give you is light." MATTHEW 11:28-30

GOD WILL SATISFY

Unscramble these Jumbles, one letter to each square, to form ordinary words. Then arrange the circled letters to solve the Mystery Answer below.

PUZZLE	ANSWER
#1 OSUIP	☐ ☐ ⊙ ☐ ☐
#2 IRYPTU	☐ ☐ ⊙ ☐ ⊙ ☐
#3 HOWWHELIRT	☐ ☐ ☐ ⊙⊙ ☐ ☐ ☐ ☐
#4 VEODTU	⊙⊙ ☐ ☐ ⊙ ☐
#5 VISTUURO	☐ ☐ ☐ ⊙ ☐ ☐ ⊙ ☐
#6 CEERRENEV	☐ ☐ ☐ ☐ ⊙ ☐ ⊙ ☐ ☐

MYSTERY ANSWER: ☐ ☐ ☐ ☐ ☐ ☐ ☐ ☐ ☐ ☐ ☐ ☐ ☐ ☐ ☐ ☐

CLUE: God's blessings come from his _____ hand.

TRIVIA: According to JesusFilm.org, nearly 250 million people have converted to Christianity after watching the *JESUS* film.

Blessed are those who hunger and thirst for righteousness, for they will be filled. MATTHEW 5:6, NIV

GOD GIVES HIS HOLY SPIRIT

Unscramble these Jumbles, one letter to each square, to form ordinary words. Then arrange the circled letters to solve the Mystery Answer below.

PUZZLE	ANSWER

#1 LAMBPASTI

#2 SHIRTCEN

#3 OREEMYNC

#4 UTRECAISH

#5 MEISINROM

#6 TRACESNAM

MYSTERY ANSWER:

CLUE: What Jesus overcame after his baptism.

TRIVIA: Most biblical baptisms were performed in rivers, such as the Jordan River.

Repent and be baptized, every one of you, in the name of Jesus Christ for the forgiveness of your sins. And you will receive the gift of the Holy Spirit. ACTS 2:38, NIV

GOD GIVES GRACE

Unscramble these Jumbles, one letter to each square, to form ordinary words. Then arrange the circled letters to solve the Mystery Answer below.

PUZZLE	ANSWER
#1 PANDOR	☐Ⓞ☐ⓄⓄ
#2 HIBELTARCA	Ⓞ☐☐ⓄⓄ☐☐☐
#3 LINNCEYE	Ⓞ☐Ⓞ☐☐Ⓞ☐
#4 PEERIVER	☐☐Ⓞ☐☐☐☐
#5 MECCLEYN	☐Ⓞ☐☐☐☐☐
#6 AMPOSOCINS	☐Ⓞ☐☐☐☐Ⓞ☐Ⓞ☐

MYSTERY ANSWER: ☐☐☐☐☐☐☐☐☐☐☐☐☐☐☐☐☐

CLUE: Jesus' offer of grace brings _____.

TRIVIA: Before Jesus' resurrection, God's people brought regular animal sacrifices to atone for their sins.

Let us come boldly to the throne of our gracious God. There we will receive his mercy, and we will find grace to help us when we need it most. HEBREWS 4:16

GOD GIVES GOOD AND PERFECT GIFTS

Unscramble these Jumbles, one letter to each square, to form ordinary words. Then arrange the circled letters to solve the Mystery Answer below.

PUZZLE	ANSWER

#1 BAREERLEPF

☐☐☐☐Ⓞ☐☐☐☐☐

#2 GNUFIND

☐☐☐☐☐Ⓞ☐

#3 FLITBUNOU

Ⓞ☐☐☐Ⓞ☐☐☐☐

#4 RADWEDA

☐☐☐Ⓞ☐☐☐

#5 SPEAKEEK

☐☐Ⓞ☐☐Ⓞ☐☐

#6 NOOSCENICS

Ⓞ☐☐☐Ⓞ☐☐☐Ⓞ☐

MYSTERY ANSWER: ☐☐☐☐☐☐☐☐☐☐☐

CLUE: **Many give gifts, but God is the ultimate _____.**

TRIVIA: Frankincense, one of the gifts of the Magi, is actually a dried resin from the *Boswellia sacra* tree, which is found in Arabia, India, and Ethiopia.

Every good and perfect gift is from above, coming down from the Father of the heavenly lights, who does not change like shifting shadows. JAMES 1:17, NIV

GOD GIVES HEALING AND SALVATION

Unscramble these Jumbles, one letter to each square, to form ordinary words. Then arrange the circled letters to solve the Mystery Answer below.

PUZZLE	ANSWER
#1 GUNIRC	☐ Ⓞ ☐ ☐ ☐ ☐
#2 LAHTEH	☐ Ⓞ ☐ ☐ ☐
#3 MYDEER	☐ ☐ ☐ Ⓞ ☐ Ⓞ
#4 SUGRNIN	Ⓞ ☐ ☐ ☐ ☐ Ⓞ
#5 NELAIGH	☐ ☐ ☐ ☐ Ⓞ ☐ ☐
#6 LENSLEWS	☐ ☐ Ⓞ ☐ Ⓞ ☐ ☐ ☐

MYSTERY ANSWER: ☐ ☐ ☐ ☐ ☐ ☐ ☐ ☐ ☐ ☐

CLUE: **God looks to save those who follow him this way.**

TRIVIA: The Bible records one instance when Jesus spat on the ground. On this occasion, he used the mud he had made to heal a blind man (see John 9).

O LORD, if you heal me, I will be truly healed; if you save me, I will be truly saved. My praises are for you alone!
JEREMIAH 17:14

198

GOD SHARES COMPLETE JOY

Unscramble these Jumbles, one letter to each square, to form ordinary words. Then arrange the circled letters to solve the Mystery Answer below.

PUZZLE	ANSWER

#1 SLUBFLIS

#2 BUELEJI

#3 RUPASLEE

#4 SENDSGAL

#5 PASHPENSI

#6 METMIRNER

MYSTERY ANSWER:

CLUE: Evidence of joy.

TRIVIA: Laughter has been found to relieve stress, increase pain tolerance, and support the immune system.

[Jesus said,] "You haven't done this before. Ask, using my name, and you will receive, and you will have abundant joy." JOHN 16:24

ANSWERS

1. **GOD SAVES CRUSHED SPIRITS**
   Jumbles: 1A—HEIGHT | 5A—RATIONAL | 6A—ERRORS | 7A—FESTIVAL
   1D—HERSELF | 2D—INTEREST | 3D—TENDS | 4D—PLAINLY
   Mystery Answer: "PAIN RELIEVER"

2. **GOD HAS GOOD PURPOSES**
   Jumbles: 1A—BABIES | 3A—RENEW | 6A—SATURDAY | 7A—PUNCH
   1D—BEAMS | 2D—BURSTING | 4D—NORTH | 5D—WEALTH
   Mystery Answer: EMPOWERING

3. **GOD HEARS HIS PEOPLE**
   Jumbles: 1A—STRESS | 4A—BROAD | 6A—LENGTHS | 7A—KINDLY
   1D—SICKLY | 2D—ROBIN | 3D—SPOTTED | 5D—DUSTY
   Mystery Answer: LISTENER

4. **GOD IS THE GIVER OF LIFE**
   Jumbles: 3A—FREEZE | 5A—ACHIEVED | 7A—DESIGNS | 8A—RUSTS
   1D—SERVANTS | 2D—MENDS | 4D—RAISINS | 6D—CLEAR
   Mystery Answer: GRATITUDE

5. **GOD WILL RESTORE YOU**
   Jumbles: 1A—CROOKED | 5A—CANAL | 6A—RESTRAIN | 7A—DEPLOYS
   1D—CLAMORED | 2D—OCCURS | 3D—KANGAROO | 4D—DOLPHINS
   Mystery Answer: COMPLAIN

6. **GOD MAKES YOU MORE THAN CONQUERORS**
   Jumbles: 1A—UNTYING | 4A—INNOCENT | 6A—EQUATOR | 7A—SMELLS
   1D—UNIVERSE | 2D—TONGUES | 3D—GENERAL | 5D—CITIES
   Mystery Answer: VICTORIOUS

7. **GOD IS FAITHFUL**
   Jumbles: 1A—FIERCELY | 5A—EVICT | 6A—PRIMES | 7A—DODGE
   1D—FOREHEAD | 2D—EQUIPPED | 3D—CONTRITE | 4D—LAZINESS
   Mystery Answer: PATIENCE

8. **GOD GRANTS REQUESTS**
   Jumbles: 1A—ORIGINAL | 4A—POSSIBLY | 6A—ENGINEER | 7A—TIMED
   1D—OPPONENT | 2D—GASOLINE | 3D—NIBBLES | 5D—YEARNS
   Mystery Answer: PROMISES

9. **GOD MAKES YOU CITIZENS OF HEAVEN**
   Jumbles: 2A—FLAGS | 5A—BORED | 6A—SQUEEZES | 7A—BRANCHES
   1D—DEBTS | 2D—FORMULA | 3D—AUDIENCE | 4D—SUPREME
   Mystery Answer: TRANSFORMED

10. **GOD REWARDS THOSE WHO PURSUE HIM**
    Jumbles: 1A—ORANGES | 5A—PERSONAL | 6A—SENTENCE | 7A—DESERTED
    1D—OPPOSED | 2D—APRON | 3D—GEOMETRY | 4D—SEARCHED
    Mystery Answer: ENTANGLEMENT

11. **GOD IS STEADFAST**
    Jumbles: 1A—POLITICS | 5A—NAMES | 6A—ADEQUATE | 7A—HONEST
    1D—PANCAKES | 2D—LUMBER | 3D—TISSUE | 4D—CAPITALS
    Mystery Answer: CONSISTENT

12. **GOD WILL REIGN FOREVER**
    Jumbles: 1A—FALLING | 4A—NOISY | 6A—EQUAL | 7A—SEEMS
    1D—FENCE | 2D—LEISURE | 3D—GIANTS | 5D—YOLKS
    Mystery Answer: GENERATION

13. **GOD CAN MAKE YOU HIS CHILDREN**
    Jumbles: 1A—SPEAKERS | 4A—MIRAGE | 6A—LIPSTICK | 7A—RESTLESS
    1D—SIMILAR | 2D—EYELINER | 3D—STRIKES | 5D—ASSET
    Mystery Answer: PEACEMAKERS

14. **GOD BLESSES SUBMISSION**
    Jumbles: 1A—INCLUDED | 5A—BOUNCE | 6A—ADEQUATE | 7A—CIRCLING
    1D—INSTANCE | 2D—CABLE | 3D—UNUSUAL | 4D—EXCITING
    Mystery Answer: INSTRUCTIONS

15. **GOD WILL KEEP YOU IN HIS HANDS**
    Jumbles: 1A—OCCUPIED | 5A—ANIMAL | 6A—ASSIST | 7A—FASTER
    1D—OPERATED | 2D—CLASSIFY | 3D—PRIESTS | 4D—DELIVER
    Mystery Answer: UNIVERSE

16. **GOD GRANTS SAFE SLEEP**
    Jumbles: 1A—TRAFFIC | 5A—AQUARIUM | 6A—CONTROL | 7A—MELODY
    1D—TRAGIC | 2D—ALUMINUM | 3D—FARMER | 4D—CHUCKLED
    Mystery Answer: TRANQUILLITY

17. **GOD PROVIDES SECURITY**
   Jumbles: 1A—SLIPPERY | 4A—EXTREME | 6A—COMPLETE |
   7A—SCOLDED
   1D—SCIENCES | 2D—REJECTED | 3D—PEELED |
   5D—TEMPO
   Mystery Answer: PROTECTION

18. **GOD KEEPS YOU ON HIS MIND**
   Jumbles: 1A—PUDDINGS | 4A—UNCOVER | 6A—ELECTED |
   7A—TIRING
   1D—PLUNGED | 2D—DOCUMENT | 3D—INVENTOR |
   5D—REDDEN
   Mystery Answer: PROVIDER

19. **GOD WILL LOVINGLY LEAD YOU**
   Jumbles: 1A—MOVIES | 4A—SHAMPOOS | 6A—INCLUDES |
   7A—SORROW
   1D—MOSQUITO | 2D—VIADUCTS | 3D—SHOULDER |
   5D—SEESAW
   Mystery Answer: SHEPHERDS

20. **GOD GIVES DIRECTION**
   Jumbles: 1A—THEATER | 5A—CRAWLED | 6A—ISSUE |
   7A—DEGREE
   1D—TICKLED | 2D—ERASING | 3D—TELLS | 4D—RIDGED
   Mystery Answer: WILDERNESS

21. **GOD HELPS US FLOURISH**
   Jumbles: 1A—PRINCE | 4A—JUMPS | 6A—CORAL |
   7A—DRIVE
   1D—POLICY | 2D—INJURED | 3D—CAMEL | 5D—SPITE
   Mystery Answer: MILLIONAIRES

22. **GOD COMPLETES HIS PERFECT WILL**
   Jumbles: 1A—FREEDOM | 5A—REFUGEE | 6A—RUINS |
   7A—EDGES
   1D—FARMING | 2D—ENFORCE | 3D—DIGGING |
   4D—MEETS
   Mystery Answer: CONFORMING

23. **GOD PROVIDES SALVATION**
   Jumbles: 1A—SLOWED | 5A—ITEMS | 6A—PRIZE |
   7A—GATES
   1D—SLIPPED | 2D—OPENING | 3D—EASIEST | 4D—STAIRS
   Mystery Answer: REDEMPTION

24. **GOD IS A SAFE HAVEN**
   Jumbles: 1A—RIVERS | 5A—CALLS | 6A—PIANO |
   7A—SHOUTED
   1D—RECIPES | 2D—VOLCANO | 3D—RESHOOT |
   4D—GUIDED
   Mystery Answer: PRESERVES

25. **GOD WELCOMES THE FAITHFUL INTO HIS
   FAMILY**
   Jumbles: 1A—WOMEN | 4A—NEWER | 6A—AREAS |
   7A—EVERY
   1D—WATCH | 2D—MANMADE | 3D—NOWHERE |
   5D—RUSTY
   Mystery Answer: CORNERSTONE

26. **GOD KEEPS US SAFE**
   Jumbles: 1A—BAKERY | 4A—CASES | 6A—LEISURE |
   7A—RIGID
   2D—KISSING | 3D—RESCUED | 4D—COLOR |
   5D—SIEGE
   Mystery Answer: CROSSING GUARD

27. **GOD EMPOWERS US**
   Jumbles: 1A—STARVED | 4A—ADDED | 6A—MOOSE |
   7A—ENDINGS
   1D—SOMEONE | 2D—ALARMED | 3D—VIDEO |
   5D—DRESS
   Mystery Answer: EVANGELISM

28. **GOD EXTENDS SACRIFICIAL LOVE**
   Jumbles: 1A—DENTAL | 4A—NARROWS | 6A—ORDER |
   7A—SYSTEMS
   1D—DANCERS | 2D—NERVOUS | 3D—ALOUD |
   5D—SORTS
   Mystery Answer: EASTER SUNDAY

29. **GOD BLESSES BELIEVERS**
   Jumbles: 1A—REPLIES | 5A—SHOWING | 6A—IMAGE |
   7A—EVENT
   1D—RESORT | 2D—PROMISE | 3D—IMITATE |
   4D—SEGMENT
   Mystery Answer: NEW TESTAMENT

30. **GOD SAVES HIS OWN**
   Jumbles: 1A—IDEAL | 4A—DUSTY | 6A—SIXTEEN |
   7A—SIGHTS
   1D—INDEX | 2D—LAYING | 3D—PAUSES | 5D—SWEPT
   Mystery Answer: LEND A HAND

31. **GOD DESTROYS THE PROUD**
   Jumbles: 1A—SUNBURN | 3A—ARRANGE | 6A—CHEWING |
   7A—SUNSET
   1D—STARCH | 2D—NERVE | 4D—NAILS | 5D—EIGHT
   Mystery Answer: HAUGHTINESS

32. **GOD PROTECTS US FROM DISASTER**
   Jumbles: 1A—AWARDED | 4A—OCTOPUS |
   6A—TORNADO | 7A—DANISH
   1D—ADOPTED | 2D—ACTOR | 3D—DISCO | 5D—PEAKS
   Mystery Answer: CHARITIES

33. **GOD EXTENDS FREEDOM**
   Jumbles: 1A—APPLAUD | 5A—VICTORY | 6A—RAISE |
   7A—EAGER
   1D—ADVERSE | 2D—PECKING | 3D—AWOKE |
   4D—DRYDOCK
   Mystery Answer: DESTROYED

34. **GOD PROTECTS US WITH ANGELS**
   Jumbles: 1A—ENGAGE | 5A—OLDER | 6A—YEARS |
   7A—NUCLEAR
   1D—EROSION | 2D—GIDDY | 3D—GARBAGE |
   4D—CLOSER
   Mystery Answer: GUARDIAN ANGEL

35. **GOD IS ALWAYS PRESENT**
   Jumbles: 1A—GRAZING | 5A—GRIEF | 6A—LEGENDS |
   7A—SACKS
   1D—GOGGLES | 2D—AGING | 3D—INFANTS |
   4D—GUESSES
   Mystery Answer: INTERCESSOR

36. **GOD LEADS HIS PEOPLE TO THEIR PROMISED
   LAND**
   Jumbles: 1A—FARAWAY | 5A—ARRIVAL | 6A—HALTS |
   7A—SHIFTY
   1D—FLASHES | 2D—RURAL | 3D—WIVES | 4D—YELLOW
   Mystery Answer: FAITHFULLY

37. GOD PROVIDES FIRM FOUNDATIONS
Jumbles: 1A—SABLES | 3A—RECITAL | 6A—ISLANDS | 7A—CITES
1D—SORTIES | 2D—EXTINCT | 4D—COLIC | 5D—LOSES
Mystery Answer: CONCRETE

38. GOD CROWNS OUR EFFORTS
Jumbles: 2A—FIFES | 5A—WAGON | 6A—RERUN | 7A—SADDLED
1D—LAWYERS | 2D—FIGURED | 3D—FUNERAL | 4D—SCORN
Mystery Answer: ENDURANCE

39. GOD DELIVERS FROM SIN
Jumbles: 1A—COMIC | 5A—ATTRACT | 6A—GOODBYE | 7A—DESIRE
1D—CHANGED | 2D—METHODS | 3D—CHAMBER | 4D—LATHER
Mystery Answer: MARY MAGDALENE

40. GOD BLESSES REVERENCE
Jumbles: 1A—REPAIRS | 3A—FASTEST | 6A—EXPRESS | 7A—GARAGES
1D—RIFLE | 2D—ICEBERG | 4D—SUPER | 5D—TESTS
Mystery Answer: SATISFIES

41. GOD IS ACCESSIBLE
Jumbles: 1A—ADVISED | 4A—SEESAWS | 6A—MERRIER | 7A—MYTHS
1D—ASSUME | 2D—SPANISH | 3D—DESERT | 5D—EARLY
Mystery Answer: MINISTERS

42. GOD GIVES GRACE
Jumbles: 1A—APPLE | 4A—TRIPPED | 6A—COCONUT | 7A—MASTERS
1D—ATTIC | 2D—PRINCES | 3D—EXPENSE | 5D—DATES
Mystery Answer: PROTESTANTISM

43. GOD ENCOURAGES US
Jumbles: 1A—THINGS | 5A—SCREW | 6A—ATHLETE | 7A—RENTED
2D—HARSH | 3D—NOWHERE | 4D—SWEDEN | 5D—STAIR
Mystery Answer: HE STRENGTHENS

44. GOD BLESSES DUTIFUL CHILDREN
Jumbles: 1A—STUDIO | 5A—TENTH | 6A—CANOE | 7A—NESTS
2D—DANGERS | 3D—OTHER | 4D—BACON | 5D—TUNES
Mystery Answer: OBEDIENCE

45. GOD OFFERS HOPE
Jumbles: 1A—ETHIC | 5A—PRIDE | 6A—ROPES | 7A—SOUNDED
1D—EFFORTS | 2D—HYPER | 3D—CLIPPED | 4D—PLEASED
Mystery Answer: SUPPORTS

46. GOD MAKES US HIS CHILDREN
Jumbles: 1A—YOUNG | 3A—AUNTS | 5A—HOUSE | 6A—MOTHERS
1D—YOUTH | 2D—SISTERS | 3D—ADULT | 4D—NIECE
Mystery Answer: RIGHTEOUS

47. GOD WILL UNITE US WITH CHRIST
Jumbles: 1A—AMBLERS | 5A—COASTAL | 6A—SADNESS | 7A—DODGED
1D—ACCUSED | 2D—BOARDED | 3D—EXTREME | 4D—SPLASH
Mystery Answer: CHARACTER

48. GOD WILL RESTORE US
Jumbles: 1A—BUSIEST | 5A—NAILING | 6A—SHELTER | 7A—ANSWER
1D—BANKS | 2D—SPIDERS | 3D—EXIST | 4D—TIGERS
Mystery Answer: INNER RENEWAL

49. GOD PREPARES US A HEAVENLY HOME
Jumbles: 1A—SILLIER | 4A—LOCKING | 6A—REALIZE | 7A—CIRCLE
1D—SOLAR | 2D—INITIAL | 3D—REGRET | 5D—CHAIR
Mystery Answer: RECLINER

50. GOD CREATES ENJOYMENT
Jumbles: 1A—RAINBOW | 4A—CRISPER | 6A—LEDGE | 7A—SILKS
1D—RECALL | 2D—ICICLES | 3D—WORKERS | 5D—PEDAL
Mystery Answer: BALLPARKS

51. GOD OFFERS A CLEAN SLATE
Jumbles: 1A—PALES | 4A—EXPLORE | 6A—EXPLAIN | 7A—TORCH
1D—PRESENT | 2D—STOMACH | 3D—CLEANED | 5D—PAPER
Mystery Answer: REPENTANCE

52. GOD LISTENS TO YOUR NEEDS
Jumbles: 1A—COMPASS | 4A—REINS | 6A—EASIEST | 7A—TROUSER
1D—CORRECT | 2D—MAIDS | 3D—ABSCESS | 5D—AFTER
Mystery Answer: COMFORTER

53. GOD HOLDS PEOPLE ACCOUNTABLE
Jumbles: 1A—FICTION | 4A—LARGE | 6A—IRELAND | 7A—GATHERS
1D—FOLDING | 2D—CURRENT | 3D—NAMED | 5D—ERASE
Mystery Answer: FALSEHOOD

54. GOD GIVES RICH BLESSINGS
Jumbles: 1A—ENTOMBS | 4A—PANCAKE | 6A—CENTURY | 7A—STYLES
1D—EXPECTS | 2D—MEASURE | 3D—SEEDY | 5D—NANNY
Mystery Answer: ABUNDANTLY

55. GOD PROTECTS HIS OWN
Jumbles: 1A—PLANTED | 5A—PHYSICS | 6A—WRONGLY | 7A—ROYAL
2D—ANYBODY | 3D—THING | 4D—DUSKY | 5D—POWER
Mystery Answer: BODYGUARD

56. GOD WILL APPEAR TO ALL
Jumbles: 1A—GRABBED | 4A—APPLIES | 6A—DRAGGED | 7A—STRAY
1D—GUARD | 2D—APPEARS | 3D—BRING | 5D—SUDSY
Mystery Answer: DEPARTURE

57. GOD DIRECTS HIS PEOPLE
Jumbles: 1A—WEALTH | 5A—RURAL | 6A—HALLWAY | 7A—SEWAGE
1D—WEIGHTS | 2D—AIRFLOW | 3D—THREW | 4D—PLOYS
Mystery Answer: RELIGIOUSLY

58. GOD DELIGHTS IN HIS CHILDREN
Jumbles: 2A—ALARM | 5A—ASSURED | 7A—HELLO | 8A—SWEETER
1D—REACHES | 3D—AIRPORT | 4D—MUDDIER | 6D—SOLVE
Mystery Answer: PLEASURE

59. GOD GIVES US A PLACE TO BELONG
Jumbles: 1A—PATTING | 4A—INDEX | 6A—YEARS | 7A—DOLES
1D—PAINT | 2D—TODAY | 3D—GROWS | 5D—X-RAYS
Mystery Answer: GOD'S DYNASTY

60. GOD EMPOWERS LEADERS
Jumbles: 1A—EXHAUST | 4A—BAKED | 6A—OUTCOME | 7A—EATEN
1D—EPITOME | 2D—HABIT | 3D—UNKNOWN | 5D—DREAM
Mystery Answer: COMMANDMENTS

61. GOD CARES FOR THE HUMBLE
Jumbles: 2A—RAZOR | 5A—DISABLE | 6A—CHINA | 7A—REGLAZE
1D—SIDECAR | 2D—RUSHING | 3D—ZEBRA | 4D—REEDS
Mystery Answer: NEBUCHADNEZZAR

62. GOD FORGETS OUR SINS
Jumbles: 1A—DEADPAN | 3A—FAVORED | 6A—ABSENCE | 7A—ROSES
1D—DEFEAT | 2D—PARENTS | 4D—VISOR | 5D—DRESS
Mystery Answer: CONFESSION

63. GOD PROVIDES ETERNAL RICHES
Jumbles: 1A—RUSSIA | 4A—HERSELF | 6A—TRAFFIC | 7A—TARTS
2D—SHELF | 3D—AFFECTS | 4D—HUTCH | 5D—REACT
Mystery Answer: TREASURE CHEST

64. GOD IS OUR CONSTANT COMPANION
Jumbles: 1A—WASTE | 3A—FAILURE | 5A—WRITERS | 6A—RIGHTLY
1D—WAITING | 2D—STUDENT | 3D—FEWER | 4D—ESSAY
Mystery Answer: STEADFAST

65. GOD HELPS US OVERCOME OUR FEARS
Jumbles: 1A—CARGO | 4A—ELECT | 6A—CAPSULE | 7A—CAVED
1D—CHEAP | 2D—OPENED | 3D—MERCY | 5D—TRUCE
Mystery Answer: ENCOURAGE

66. GOD DESIRES TO BE CLOSE TO YOU
Jumbles: 1A—ELBOWS | 4A—HUNTERS | 6A—BELTS | 7A—TOSSING
1D—EXHIBIT | 2D—BUNDLES | 3D—WEEKS | 5D—SWING
Mystery Answer: GODLINESS

67. GOD LOVES INFINITELY THROUGH CHRIST
Jumbles: 1A—KNEES | 4A—THANK | 6A—EXPECTS | 7A—SHEDS
1D—KITTENS | 2D—EXAMPLE | 3D—INVESTS | 5D—KICKS
Mystery Answer: EPHESIANS

68. GOD GIVES EVERLASTING LIFE
Jumbles: 1A—SEWED | 5A—NAILS | 6A—MONSTER | 7A—DEMAND
1D—SYNONYM | 2D—WRITTEN | 3D—DESIRE | 4D—SEEMED
Mystery Answer: EYEWITNESSES

69. GOD GRANTS SUCCESS
Jumbles: 1A—APPROVE | 5A—AGENT | 6A—DESPAIR | 7A—DECIDED
1D—AWARDED | 2D—POETS | 3D—OUTWARD | 4D—ENTERED
Mystery Answer: DEVOTIONS

70. GOD OFFERS PEACE
Jumbles: 2A—PSALM | 4A—ALTAR | 6A—TORAH | 7A—SIMON
1D—CHAPTER | 2D—PETER | 3D—ABRAHAM | 5D—SATAN
Mystery Answer: CHAMPION

71. GOD PROVIDES FAMILIES
Jumbles: 2A—REFER | 5A—RIDER | 6A—PRODUCT | 7A—NICETY
1D—SCRAP | 2D—RADIO | 3D—FORTUNE | 4D—RIGHTLY
Mystery Answer: GRANDFATHER

72. GOD PROLONGS LIFE
Jumbles: 1A—TEETH | 4A—GOOSE | 5A—GUEST | 6A—ESTATE
1D—THOUGHT | 2D—ELEMENT | 3D—HAUNTS | 4D—GABLE
Mystery Answer: METHUSELAH

73. GOD CALMS FEARS
Jumbles: 1A—ADOPTED | 4A—REVEALS | 6A—WINTERS | 7A—NESTS
1D—ARROW | 2D—TRAVELS | 3D—DISKS | 5D—VENUS
Mystery Answer: NERVOUSNESS

74. GOD IS ALWAYS WITH US
Jumbles: 1A—MUSIC | 5A—SWELL | 6A—APPEARS | 7A—ELDEST
1D—MESSAGE | 2D—STEPPED | 3D—COLLARS | 4D—PLAYS
Mystery Answer: LAST SUPPER

75. GOD IS OUR HEAVENLY FATHER
Jumbles: 1A—SKILL | 5A—READERS | 6A—POPULAR | 7A—SADDLE
1D—SNAPPED | 2D—IDEAL | 3D—LOSER | 4D—GRAPES
Mystery Answer: PRODIGAL SON

76. GOD REMOVES DISGRACE
Jumbles: 1A—YACHT | 4A—WORKMAN | 6A—ILLNESS | 7A—EGYPT
2D—COMMENT | 3D—TUNES | 4D—WHILE | 5D—RELAY
Mystery Answer: SYMPATHY

77. GOD IS OUR KNOWABLE CREATOR
Jumbles: 1A—LABOR | 5A—PALACES | 6A—POINTER | 7A—MODEM
2D—BELGIUM | 3D—RECITED | 4D—ROSTRUM | 5D—PIPES
Mystery Answer: COMMUNE

78. GOD STRENGTHENS US
Jumbles: 1A—SUFFER | 4A—RUNNING | 6A—PERFUME | 7A—HEELS
2D—FAILURE | 3D—RIGGERS | 4D—REPLY | 5D—NORTH
Mystery Answer: LIMITLESS

79. GOD STEERS US FROM TEMPTATION
Jumbles: 1A—BREAKS | 4A—KNOBS | 6A—IMMENSE | 7A—GESTURE
1D—BUZZING | 2D—ESKIMOS | 3D—KNOWN | 5D—SCENE
Mystery Answer: ENCOURAGEMENT

80. GOD IS PLEASED BY OUR GOOD WORKS
Jumbles: 1A—SUMMIT | 4A—HUDDLED | 6A—TUMMY | 7A—DESERVE
2D—MILKY | 3D—TADPOLE | 4D—HATED | 5D—DOMES
Mystery Answer: HOSPITALITY

81. GOD NOURISHES SOULS
Jumbles: 1A—REDUCE | 5A—LIMIT | 6A—TENTH | 7A—DISLIKE
1D—RELATED | 2D—DEMANDS | 3D—CATCH | 4D—TANGLE
Mystery Answer: HUMANITARIAN

82. GOD FORGIVES
Jumbles: 1A—VAPOR | 5A—TROUBLE | 6A—MASSIVE | 7A—NAUGHT
1D—VITAMIN | 2D—POOLS | 3D—RUBBISH | 4D—SCENES
Mystery Answer: TRANSGRESS

83. GOD HELPS US LIVE IN PEACE
Jumbles: 1A—PACKED | 4A—MAGIC | 6A—CORDS | 7A—SALTY
1D—PARSONS | 2D—COMICAL | 3D—EAGERLY | 5D—CASES
Mystery Answer: GOOD SAMARITAN

84. GOD PROVIDES POWER
Jumbles: 1A—DESERTS | 4A—ANSWERS | 6A—ERASE | 7A—DATES
1D—DEARLY | 2D—SUSPEND | 3D—SYSTEMS | 5D—EXACT
Mystery Answer: MUSTARD SEED

85. GOD PERMITS CONSEQUENCES FOR OUR ACTIONS
Jumbles: 1A—WHISKER | 5A—LISTENS | 6A—OPENING | 7A—ENERGY
1D—WELCOME | 2D—ISSUE | 3D—KEEPING | 4D—RESIGN
Mystery Answer: REPERCUSSIONS

86. GOD IS NEAR
Jumbles: 2A—CHILD | 5A—SERVE | 6A—GLASSES | 7A—SUNSET
1D—DESIGNS | 2D—CURTAIN | 3D—IDEAS | 4D—DANISH
Mystery Answer: CHALLENGES

87. GOD KEEPS US ACCOUNTABLE
Jumbles: 1A—SECONDS | 5A—RINGING | 6A—ITALY | 7A—GATES
1D—SORTING | 2D—CONTACT | 3D—NOISY | 4D—SIGNAL
Mystery Answer: INTEGRITY

88. GOD HONORS THE RIGHTEOUS
Jumbles: 1A—PRAISED | 5A—SHOWS | 6A—FOALS | 7A—CINEMAS
1D—PACIFIC | 2D—ABSTAIN | 3D—SHOPS | 4D—DISCUSS
Mystery Answer: FRIENDSHIP

89. GOD EMBRACES US AS FAMILY
Jumbles: 1A—REMAIN | 5A—ADAPT | 6A—INNER | 7A—DEGREES
1D—REACHED | 2D—MEANING | 3D—INTENSE | 4D—LEARNS
Mystery Answer: INHERITANCE

90. GOD SUSTAINS DURING FAMINE
Jumbles: 1A—CONIC | 5A—PAINTER | 6A—EFFORTS | 7A—ROYAL
1D—CHIEFLY | 2D—NATURAL | 3D—CARESS | 4D—APPEAR
Mystery Answer: FERTILE CRESCENT

91. GOD BLESSES THE FAITHFUL
Jumbles: 1A—SIGHT | 4A—NOOSE | 6A—ALIEN | 7A—ENEMIES
1D—SAUSAGE | 2D—GENUINE | 3D—THORN | 5D—EDGES
Mystery Answer: MOUNTAINS

92. GOD GIVES NEW BEGINNINGS
Jumbles: 1A—ITALICS | 5A—SHOWN | 6A—CLEARER | 7A—SPEND
1D—INSECTS | 2D—AWOKE | 3D—IGNORED | 4D—SALARY
Mystery Answer: [W]IPES [T]HE [S]LATE [C]LEAN

93. GOD REWARDS HUMILITY
Jumbles: 1A—KETCHUP | 4A—TROLLEY | 6A—HOSTAGE | 7A—NURSE
1D—KITCHEN | 2D—TROTS | 3D—PAYMENT | 5D—LEAVE
Mystery Answer: TURN [THE] OTHER CHEEK

94. GOD DELIVERS FROM ENEMIES
Jumbles: 1A—DIRTIER | 4A—REMARKS | 6A—INVADES | 7A—GALLOPS
1D—DARLING | 2D—REMOVAL | 3D—RISES | 5D—RADIO
Mystery Answer: PROMISED LAND

95. GOD HAS COMPASSION FOR YOUR SORROWS
Jumbles: 1A—CUBIC | 4A—OWNER | 5A—BUFFALO | 6A—PARENTS
1D—CLIMB | 2D—CONTAIN | 3D—PERSONS | 4D—OFFER
Mystery Answer: LONELINESS

96. GOD PROTECTS YOU FROM PERIL
Jumbles: 1A—BESIDES | 5A—CARGO | 6A—RHYME | 7A—EDDIES
1D—BALANCE | 2D—SECURED | 3D—DIRTY | 4D—STORES
Mystery Answer: DANGEROUS

97. GOD IS NEAR
Jumbles: 2A—SERUM | 5A—RULED | 6A—NEEDS | 7A—MASTER
1D—FIEFDOM | 2D—STRANDS | 3D—RELIEVE | 4D—MODEST
Mystery Answer: IMMANUEL

98. GOD PROVIDES REDEMPTION
Jumbles: 1A—PATCHES | 5A—LUGGAGE | 6A—SERVING | 7A—STAYS
1D—POLISH | 2D—TIGER | 3D—HEAVILY | 4D—SLEDGE
Mystery Answer: SUPERSEDES

99. GOD WILL BE EXALTED AROUND THE WORLD
Jumbles: 1A—AMUSING | 3A—RESTORE | 6A—RACKS | 7A—NEWER
1D—AFRICAN | 2D—GREASY | 4D—SCREW | 5D—OCCUR
Mystery Answer: MISSIONARY

100. GOD ANSWERS PRAYER
Jumbles: 1A—COLORS | 5A—RINDS | 6A—ADDRESS | 7A—NIGHTLY
1D—CURTAIN | 2D—LINED | 3D—RESPECT | 4D—MARSHY
Mystery Answer: MORNING PRAYER

101. GOD WILL ALWAYS BE WITH YOU
Jumbles: 1A—BEAUTY | 4A—KINDNESS | 6A—TASTE | 7A—DONKEYS
1D—BLIZZARD | 2D—ADDITION | 3D—TREASURE | 5D—SPENDS
Mystery Answer: INSEPARABLE

102. GOD ALLEVIATES PAIN
Jumbles: 1A—WORST | 4A—LIQUIDS | 6A—ELVES |
7A—GREASE
1D—WALKING | 2D—THIEVES | 3D—POSES |
5D—QUEUE
Mystery Answer: TEARDROPS

103. GOD IS GOOD TO ALL
Jumbles: | 2A—ROBBERS | 5A—ADAPTING |
6A—STITCHES | 7A—HIGHLY
1D—VERTICAL | 2D—ROARS | 3D—BLAZING |
4D—SINGER
Mystery Answer: CELEBRATION

104. GOD INSTILLS PEACE
Jumbles: 1A—WORSHIP | 5A—TEASPOON | 6A—STING |
7A—CONQUEST
1D—WATERS | 2D—REACTION | 3D—HOPING |
4D—PRONOUNS
Mystery Answer: COUNTENANCE

105. GOD WILL KEEP HIS PROMISES
Jumbles: 1A—SWALLOWS | 5A—ORCHARDS |
6A—STATIONS | 7A—TANKS
1D—SPOONS | 2D—AIRCRAFT | 3D—LOCATION |
4D—WEDDINGS
Mystery Answer: ADORATION

106. GOD WILL DELIVER ON HIS INTENTIONS
Jumbles: 1A—TOUCHES | 5A—SPAIN | 6A—CHIMNEYS |
7A—LESSONS
1D—TROPICAL | 2D—UPSTAIRS | 3D—HEAVEN |
4D—SYNONYMS
Mystery Answer: ACCOMPLISH

107. GOD IS A COMPASSIONATE FATHER
Jumbles: 1A—RECKON | 3A—SENSIBLE | 6A—METALLIC |
7A—LOWLANDS
1D—RESEMBLE | 2D—NIBBLING | 4D—SNAIL |
5D—EXCUSE
Mystery Answer: ABANDONMENT

108. GOD PROVIDES ENDURING LOVE
Jumbles: 1A—DESCRIBE | 4A—UNTIL | 6A—TRUSTED |
7A—UNKNOWN
1D—DOUBTFUL | 2D—RELATION | 3D—BREEDING |
5D—TRUNK
Mystery Answer: ATTENTION

109. GOD WILL NEVER FORSAKE YOU
Jumbles: | 3A—ANYHOW | 5A—BRANCHES |
7A—EXPLORES | 8A—WILDEST
1D—BAUBLE | 2D—THESES | 4D—HANDLED |
6D—HURTS
Mystery Answer: TRUSTWORTHY

110. GOD LIFTS BURDENS
Jumbles: 1A—ESCAPES | 5A—THURSDAY |
6A—MAGNETIC | 7A—THOROUGH
1D—ESTIMATE | 2D—CLUNG | 3D—PASTE |
4D—SCARING
Mystery Answer: COUNSELOR

111. GOD IS A FORTRESS
Jumbles: 1A—ANCHORED | 5A—SOUNDING |
6A—TRAINS | 7A—DELAYED
1D—ASSIGNED | 2D—CAUGHT | 3D—ORDINARY |
4D—DIGITS
Mystery Answer: STRONGHOLD

112. GOD REWARDS THE HUMBLE
Jumbles: 1A—LAMPS | 4A—CRADLES | 6A—SANDAL |
7A—SURVIVED
1D—LUCKIEST | 2D—MEANS | 3D—SPLENDID |
5D—SHADE
Mystery Answer: HANDMAIDEN

113. GOD WILL GIVE TO THOSE WHO SEEK HIM
Jumbles: 1A—CRAYON | 4A—MILITARY | 6A—LONGING |
7A—EXCUSES
1D—COMPLETE | 2D—ATLANTIC | 3D—OUTLINES |
5D—ROGUES
Mystery Answer: STRUGGLES

114. GOD GIVES HOPE TO THE DESPONDENT
Jumbles: 1A—ACROBAT | 4A—SECRETLY | 6A—ASHORE |
7A—URGED
1D—ASSEMBLY | 2D—RACIAL | 3D—ALTHOUGH |
5D—YIELD
Mystery Answer: BEARABLE

115. GOD WILL HELP YOU GUARD YOUR HEARTS
Jumbles: 1A—BOTTOMS | 4A—CREDIT | 5A—NUISANCE |
6A—SUPPOSED
1D—BANANAS | 2D—OPERATOR | 3D—SNITCHES |
4D—CRISP
Mystery Answer: CONCENTRATION

116. GOD WATCHES OVER YOU
Jumbles: 1A—NATURES | 5A—EVIDENT | 6A—FORGIVEN |
7A—KEEPS
1D—NOTEBOOK | 2D—TRYING | 3D—RECEIVES |
4D—SEATING
Mystery Answer: TRANSPARENT

117. GOD CAN RESCUE THE TROUBLED
Jumbles: 1A—PROPERLY | 4A—EXERCISE |
6A—TREMBLED | 7A—ROADSIDE
1D—PRETTIER | 2D—OBEYED | 3D—LISTENED |
5D—CABLES
Mystery Answer: LIBERATION

118. GOD GIVES CONSOLATION AND JOY
Jumbles: 1A—CLASSIC | 4A—AGREE | 6A—HISTORIC |
7A—NEEDING
1D—CRASHING | 2D—ARRESTED | 3D—CARRIAGE |
5D—EXOTIC
Mystery Answer: DISTRESSED

119. GOD OFFERS PERMANENT LOVE
Jumbles: 1A—NECKLACE | 4A—RAINFALL | 6A—EVENT |
7A—FROST
1D—NORTHERN | 2D—CRICKET | 3D—CULTURES |
5D—FATTER
Mystery Answer: FAITHFUL

120. GOD EMBRACES YOU
Jumbles: | 3A—DRIER | 4A—REPUBLIC | 5A—BALLOONS |
6A—SLIDES
1D—MILLIONS | 2D—PRICES | 3D—DOUBLED |
4D—ROBES
Mystery Answer: INNER PEACE

121. GOD WILL STAY WITH YOU
Jumbles: 1A—RIBBONS | 4A—FASTENS | 6A—ROUND |
7A—ENTERED
1D—REFEREE | 2D—BISCUIT | 3D—SUSPEND |
5D—ELDER
Mystery Answer: SUSTAINER

122. GOD REPAYS GOOD WORKS
Jumbles: 2A—ROPES | 4A—SENDING | 6A—OMITTED | 7A—EAGERLY
1D—RESTORE | 2D—RINGING | 3D—PAINTER | 5D—GIDDY
Mystery Answer: GENEROSITY

123. GOD OFFERS FREEDOM FROM FEAR
Jumbles: 1A—GLANCED | 4A—FREEDOM | 6A—SESSION | 7A—ALWAYS
1D—GIFTS | 2D—AREAS | 3D—DEMAND | 5D—DAISY
Mystery Answer: FEARLESS

124. GOD PROSPERS HIS OWN
Jumbles: 1A—PLASTIC | 5A—SECTION | 6A—USELESS | 7A—ENTRIES
1D—PASTURE | 2D—ANCIENT | 3D—TRIBE | 4D—CONES
Mystery Answer: BLUEPRINT

125. GOD CREATES HEAVENLY HOMES
Jumbles: 1A—SCIENCE | 5A—UPSET | 6A—DREAD | 7A—DETAILS
1D—SOUNDED | 2D—INSPECT | 3D—NOTED | 4D—EXCUSES
Mystery Answer: LUXURIES

126. GOD PROMISES WE WILL NEVER BE ALONE
Jumbles: 1A—EXPOSED | 5A—STORAGE | 6A—NAUGHTS | 7A—SMELLED
2D—PRODUCE | 3D—SMASH | 4D—DRESSED | 5D—SINKS
Mystery Answer: HIS PRESENCE

127. GOD GUIDES HIS OWN
Jumbles: 1A—SECRET | 4A—ANNOYED | 6A—TWIST | 7A—DOGGING
1D—STARTED | 2D—CUNNING | 3D—EGYPT | 5D—DEBUG
Mystery Answer: GUIDEPOSTS

128. GOD IS FAITHFUL
Jumbles: 1A—LOWBOY | 4A—CASTING | 6A—EVENT | 7A—SUNDAES
1D—LOCATES | 2D—WESTERN | 3D—OVINE | 5D—GATES
Mystery Answer: CONSTANT

129. GOD IS A LOVING FATHER
Jumbles: 1A—HANGING | 5A—AMERICA | 6A—LEARN | 7A—GASPED
1D—HEARING | 2D—NEEDLES | 3D—IMITATE | 4D—GRAINS
Mystery Answer: CHILDREN

130. GOD BLESSES GODLY WOMEN
Jumbles: 1A—BASKETS | 5A—FALSE | 6A—ANIMALS | 7A—OUGHT
1D—BUFFALO | 2D—SELLING | 3D—ELEGANT | 4D—SQUASH
Mystery Answer: FASHIONABLE

131. GOD CAN HELP US LIVE WITHOUT WANT
Jumbles: 1A—BECAUSE | 4A—TITLE | 6A—LIZARDS | 7A—SANDY
1D—BATTLES | 2D—CITIZEN | 3D—UTTERLY | 5D—EASEL
Mystery Answer: DAILY BREAD

132. GOD CAN GRANT LONG LIFE
Jumbles: 1A—EMBASSY | 4A—ENGINES | 6A—EQUAL | 7A—EXTENDS
1D—EXECUTE | 2D—BIGGEST | 3D—SUNBURN | 5D—SALES
Mystery Answer: CENTENARIANS

133. GOD BLESSES OUR GIVING
Jumbles: 1A—POINTED | 5A—DANCE | 6A—LARGE | 7A—DEVISED
1D—PADDLED | 2D—INNER | 3D—THEME | 4D—DEPTH
Mystery Answer: PHILANTHROPIST

134. GOD GIVES FULLNESS OF LIFE
Jumbles: 1A—FAITHFUL | 5A—RETURN | 6A—RAINED | 7A—ENOUGH
1D—FURROWED | 2D—INTERIOR | 3D—HURTING | 4D—LIVIDLY
Mystery Answer: OVERFLOWING

135. GOD MEETS WITH HIS PEOPLE
Jumbles: 1A—COALS | 5A—RATIO | 6A—VIOLINS | 7A—SIGNS
1D—CARAVAN | 2D—AUTHORS | 3D—SNOWING | 4D—GROUSES
Mystery Answer: CONGREGATION

136. GOD DRIES OUR TEARS
Jumbles: 1A—ORANGES | 5A—TEMPO | 6A—INTENSE | 7A—ENCASED
1D—OUTSIDE | 2D—ADMIT | 3D—GROUNDS | 4D—SEAWEED
Mystery Answer: COMPASSION

137. GOD RENEWS OUR STRENGTH
Jumbles: 1A—REDUCE | 5A—LAUGH | 6A—ANGRIER | 7A—SATISFY
1D—REVEALS | 2D—DELIGHT | 3D—COUSINS | 4D—THORNY
Mystery Answer: REFRESHES

138. GOD CHOOSES HIS OWN
Jumbles: 1A—PAINTER | 5A—ROOFS | 6A—INSTEAD | 7A—STEPPED
1D—PARTIES | 2D—IRONS | 3D—TASTE | 4D—ROUNDED
Mystery Answer: DESTINATION

139. GOD IS OUR ETERNAL GUIDE
Jumbles: 1A—BANDAGE | 4A—SORTIES | 6A—OWNED | 7A—GASES
1D—BASKING | 2D—NERVOUS | 3D—ALIGN | 5D—SIDLE
Mystery Answer: EVERLASTING

140. GOD IS APPROACHABLE
Jumbles: 1A—RARELY | 4A—VACUOUS | 6A—DISLIKE | 7A—RIDGES
1D—RAVED | 2D—RICES | 3D—LOOKING | 5D—SEEPS
Mystery Answer: [THE] LORD'S PRAYER

141. GOD WILL JUDGE OUR ACTIONS
Jumbles: 1A—UPSIDE | 4A—PHONING | 6A—EXTRA | 7A—SPADES
1D—UPPER | 2D—STOLE | 3D—DRIFTED | 5D—GOATS
Mystery Answer: RIGHTEOUSNESS

142. GOD PROVIDES VICTORY
Jumbles: 1A—ACCUSER | 4A—TRACTOR | 6A—INCLINE | 7A—SIGHS

1D—ATTAIN | 2D—CHANCES | 3D—SETTING | 5D—REELS
Mystery Answer: RESURRECTION

143. GOD'S LOVE IS UNFAILING
Jumbles: 1A—REBUTS | 5A—THREE | 6A—ELASTIC |
7A—TANDEM
1D—RETREAT | 2D—BARGAIN | 3D—TREAT | 4D—DANCE
Mystery Answer: A TENDER HEART

144. GOD WILL COMPLETE OUR GROWTH
Jumbles: 1A—PEAKS | 3A—FLOWING | 5A—IRONS |
6A—DEEPEST
1D—PROPOSE | 2D—SEGMENT | 3D—FRIED | 4D—ISSUE
Mystery Answer: A WORK IN PROGRESS

145. GOD OFFERS ABUNDANT GRACE
Jumbles: 1A—ADVERBS | 4A—PAINFUL | 6A—EMERGED |
7A—FOSTER
1D—APPLE | 2D—REFUGEE | 3D—SALADS | 5D—ITEMS
Mystery Answer: PARDONABLE

146. GOD GIVES SHELTER FROM TROUBLE
Jumbles: 1A—REVEALS | 5A—SILKS | 6A—LEARNED |
7A—SINGERS

1D—RESULTS | 2D—VILLAIN | 3D—ABSENCE |
4D—SOUND
Mystery Answer: TENDER LOVING CARE

147. GOD WILL PUNISH THE WICKED
Jumbles: 1A—ITALIAN | 5A—VOCAL | 6A—HANGS |
7A—DOLLS
1D—INVADED | 2D—ALCOHOL | 3D—ISLANDS |
4D—NICKS
Mystery Answer: VINDICATION

148. GOD DISCIPLINES THE ARROGANT
Jumbles: 1A—EXPUNGE | 4A—HANDCUFF |
6A—INSTANCE | 7A—ECHOES
1D—ETHNIC | 2D—PUNISHED | 3D—EFFECTED |
5D—CLASH
Mystery Answer: CONFIDENCE

149. GOD WILL CREATE A NEW ORDER
Jumbles: 1A—PEELINGS | 4A—ATTACKED | 6A—TUNING |
7A—COMMONLY
1D—PLASTIC | 2D—EATEN | 3D—SIDEWAYS |
5D—CANNON
Mystery Answer: SECOND COMING

SUPER JUMBLES

150. GOD'S PEOPLE THRIVE
Jumbles: 1. OLIVES | 2. GRAINS | 3. HARVEST |
4. RAINFALL | 5. PASTURES | 6. PROSPERITY
Mystery Answer: FERVENT

151. GOD RESTORES HEALTH
Jumbles: 1. FITNESS | 2. RECOVER | 3. THERAPY |
4. HEALTHY | 5. VITALITY | 6. WELL-BEING
Mystery Answer: FLOWERS

152. GOD DEVELOPS OUR CHARACTER
Jumbles: 1. FAITHFULNESS | 2. LOVING | 3. JOYFUL |
4. PATIENCE | 5. PEACEFUL | 6. GOODNESS
Mystery Answer: JUNGLE

153. GOD EMBRACES HIS FAMILY
Jumbles: 1. BROOD | 2. FAMILY | 3. HERITAGE |
4. LINEAGE | 5. HOUSEHOLD | 6. OFFSPRING
Mystery Answer: BELONG

154. GOD GRANTS SAFETY
Jumbles: 1. OASIS | 2. HAVEN | 3. REFUGE | 4. HARBOR |
5. SHELTER | 6. RETREAT
Mystery Answer: FATHER

155. GOD FORGIVES SINS
Jumbles: 1. SNOWFALL | 2. IVORY | 3. GLOWING |
4. SPOTLESS | 5. GLEANING | 6. INNOCENT
Mystery Answer: WOOLLY

156. GOD HEALS
Jumbles: 1. TONIC | 2. DOCTOR | 3. REPAIRED | 4. PATCHY |
5. BANDAGE | 6. MEDICINE
Mystery Answer: PRIMARY

157. GOD COMFORTS
Jumbles: 1. CHEER | 2. SOOTHE | 3. SOLACE |
4. REFRESHED | 5. GLADDEN | 6. CONSOLATION
Mystery Answer: FRAGRANCE

158. GOD DEFENDS
Jumbles: 1. STRUGGLE | 2. GUARDIAN | 3. DEFENDER |
4. PROTECTION | 5. CHAIN MAIL | 6. ADVOCATE
Mystery Answer: VANGUARD

159. GOD ANSWERS PRAYERS
Jumbles: 1. GRANTED | 2. CONFIRM | 3. PROVIDE |
4. FULFILL | 5. SATISFY | 6. RESPONDED
Mystery Answer: LOVINGLY

160. GOD IS OUR ADVOCATE
Jumbles: 1. FAVORITE | 2. DEFEND | 3. SUPPORT |
4. PROTECTOR | 5. COUNSEL | 6. PROMOTE
Mystery Answer: PROPONENT

161. GOD SACRIFICED FOR US
Jumbles: 1. YIELDING | 2. DEVOTE | 3. MARTYRDOM |
4. FORFEIT | 5. ENDURED | 6. OFFERING
Mystery Answer: OVERTURNED

162. GOD BLESSES HIS CHILDREN
Jumbles: 1. CROPS | 2. FRUIT FLY | 3. GLEANING |
4. AUTUMN | 5. GATHERING | 6. HARVESTER
Mystery Answer: LETTUCE

163. GOD GIVES INSIGHT
Jumbles: 1. LEARNING | 2. WISDOM | 3. VISIONARY |
4. INSIGHT | 5. SCHOLARS | 6. DISCRIMINATE
Mystery Answer: VOICE MAIL

164. **GOD EXTENDS COMPASSION**
Jumbles: 1. MERCIFUL | 2. GRACIOUS | 3. WARMTH |
4. REMORSE | 5. CHARITY | 6. SYMPATHY
Mystery Answer: EPHRAIM

165. **GOD PROVIDES FREEDOM**
Jumbles: 1. LIBERTY | 2. LEISURE | 3. RELEASE |
4. IMMUNITY | 5. PRIVILEGE | 6. AUTONOMY
Mystery Answer: ETERNITY

166. **GOD IS OUR ROCK**
Jumbles: 1. REFUGE | 2. SHIELDED | 3. COMFORTER |
4. SECURITY | 5. RELIEVING | 6. PROTECTION
Mystery Answer: FIREFIGHTERS

167. **GOD PROVIDES STRENGTH**
Jumbles: 1. AUTHORITY | 2. POWERFUL | 3. VIGOROUS |
4. MUSCLE | 5. ENERGIZES | 6. MOMENTUM
Mystery Answer: OUTWEIGHS

168. **GOD SENDS GUARDIAN ANGELS**
Jumbles: 1. WATCHER | 2. DEFENDS | 3. BUMPERS |
4. ESCORTING | 5. WATCHTOWER | 6. PATROLLING
Mystery Answer: CHERUBIM

169. **GOD MAKES US NEW CREATIONS**
Jumbles: 1. REGENERATE | 2. NATURAL | 3. RENEWAL |
4. REFRESH | 5. ORIGINAL | 6. RESTORE
Mystery Answer: FORGOTTEN

170. **GOD EXTENDS HIS HOLINESS**
Jumbles: 1. ELECTED | 2. SACREDNESS | 3. CHOICE |
4. VENERATED | 5. DEVOTED | 6. REVERENT
Mystery Answer: RECONCILED

171. **GOD GIVES PERSEVERANCE**
Jumbles: 1. ADVERSITY | 2. STAMINA | 3. PERSISTENCE |
4. PATIENCE | 5. TENACIOUS | 6. DOGGEDNESS
Mystery Answer: IDENTITY

172. **GOD RESTORES HIS PEOPLE**
Jumbles: 1. STALWART | 2. UNYIELDING | 3. RECLAIMED |
4. STEADIES | 5. SECURELY | 6. REBUILDING
Mystery Answer: SURGERY

173. **GOD IS ACCESSIBLE**
Jumbles: 1. CORDIAL | 2. SORROWFUL | 3. EMPATHY |
4. HARMONIZE | 5. AFFINITY | 6. KINDNESS
Mystery Answer: DOORWAY

174. **GOD MEETS NEEDS**
Jumbles: 1. ECLIPSED | 2. ENDOWED | 3. RENDERED |
4. SATISFIED | 5. NOURISH | 6. REPLENISH
Mystery Answer: SUPPLIER

175. **GOD GIVES PURPOSE**
Jumbles: 1. DESIGNED | 2. INTENTION | 3. REASONS |
4. MISSION | 5. FUNCTION | 6. AMBITION
Mystery Answer: TIMING

176. **GOD STRENGTHENS WITH COURAGE**
Jumbles: 1. INTREPID | 2. BRAVADO | 3. GALLANT |
4. COURAGEOUS | 5. FEARLESS | 6. ADVENTUROUS
Mystery Answer: BOLDNESS

177. **GOD KEEPS HIS PROMISES**
Jumbles: 1. POSSIBILITY | 2. POTENTIAL | 3. ASSURANCE |
4. PROMISED | 5. GUARANTEE | 6. COMMITTED
Mystery Answer: AGREEMENT

178. **GOD GIVES PROSPERITY**
Jumbles: 1. THRIVES | 2. BURGEONS | 3. SUCCEEDS |
4. FLOURISH | 5. PROGRESS | 6. ABUNDANT
Mystery Answer: PROVISION

TRIVIA JUMBLES

179. **GOD SUSTAINS US**
Jumbles: 1. HUNGRY | 2. TRUSTING | 3. PLENTY |
4. THIRSTY | 5. PROVISION | 6. ABUNDANCE
Mystery Answer: NUTRITION
Trivia Answer: ON AVERAGE, MEN NEED 10–12 GLASSES
AND WOMEN NEED 8–10 GLASSES PER DAY.

180. **GOD ABOUNDS IN LOVE**
Jumbles: 1. GENTLE | 2. PATIENTS | 3. FAITHFUL |
4. MERCIFUL | 5. GRACIOUS | 6. PROFOUND
Mystery Answer: ISRAELITES
Trivia Answer: ISRAEL

181. **GOD PROVIDES TEACHERS**
Jumbles: 1. PRIDEFUL | 2. ELDERS | 3. SUBMIT |
4. MODESTY | 5. HUMILITY | 6. MEEKNESS
Mystery Answer: MENTOR
Trivia Answer: ELI

182. **GOD OFFERS PERFECT PEACE**
Jumbles: 1. LIFELONG | 2. ETERNAL | 3. FOREVER |
4. MINDFUL | 5. PERMANENT | 6. STEADFAST
Mystery Answer: PROMISES
Trivia Answer: SHALOM

183. **GOD GIVES HEAVENLY REWARD**
Jumbles: 1. CRUCIFY | 2. SUFFER | 3. VICTIM |
4. TORMENT | 5. TORTURE | 6. PERSECUTE
Mystery Answer: FUTURE
Trivia Answer: CHURCH TRADITION SAYS THAT PETER WAS
MARTYRED THIS WAY.

184. **GOD SECURES VICTORY**
Jumbles: 1. GLORIOUS | 2. TRIUMPH | 3. VICTORY |
4. CONQUER | 5. SUCCEED | 6. OVERCOME
Mystery Answer: SUPERIOR
Trivia Answer: GOLIATH

185. **GOD GRANTS DREAMS**
Jumbles: 1. VISIONARY | 2. WISHES | 3. LONGING |
4. PASSION | 5. DREAMING | 6. YEARNING
Mystery Answer: IMAGINE
Trivia Answer: TO MEET THE CHRIST CHILD BEFORE HE DIED

186. **GOD PROVIDES HEAVENLY RICHES**
Jumbles: 1. WEALTHIER | 2. RICHEST | 3. INHERITED |
4. CAPITAL | 5. FORTUNE | 6. BOUNTIES
Mystery Answer: PERISHABLE
Trivia Answer: KING SOLOMON

187. GOD MENDS HEARTS
Jumbles: 1. ATTACHE | 2. REPARTEE | 3. REBUILT | 4. IMPROVE | 5. RESTORE | 6. ALLEVIATE
Mystery Answer: CHEERS UP
Trivia Answer: JESUS WEPT WITH MARY AND MARTHA AT LAZARUS'S GRAVESIDE BEFORE RAISING HIM FROM THE DEAD.

188. GOD GRANTS PEACE
Jumbles: 1. PLACID | 2. SERENELY | 3. RELAXED | 4. CONTENTED | 5. CALMNESS | 6. TRANQUILLY
Mystery Answer: CANDLES
Trivia Answer: THIS FAMOUS CHRISTMAS PHRASE WAS FIRST SAID BY THE ANGELS THAT ANNOUNCED JESUS' BIRTH TO NEARBY SHEPHERDS.

189. GOD BEARS OUR BURDENS
Jumbles: 1. HEAVINESS | 2. COLOSSAL | 3. BURDENED | 4. TROUBLED | 5. UNWIELDY | 6. CUMBERSOME
Mystery Answer: MUSCULARITY
Trivia Answer: THREE: SKELETAL, SMOOTH, AND CARDIAC

190. GOD IS COMMITTED TO YOU
Jumbles: 1. PLEDGES | 2. TREATY | 3. COVENANT | 4. DEVOTION | 5. CONTRACT | 6. AGREEMENT
Mystery Answer: MARRIAGE

191. GOD CARES FOR CREATION
Jumbles: 1. WORRYING | 2. GREENER | 3. BEHOLD | 4. ATTENDANT | 5. CONCERN | 6. INTEREST
Mystery Answer: HONEYBEE

192. GOD PARTNERS WITH US
Jumbles: 1. CLOSELY | 2. TANDEM | 3. NEARBY | 4. BESIDE | 5. ADJOIN | 6. ACCOMPANY
Mystery Answer: COMPANION

193. GOD GIVES REST
Jumbles: 1. CATNAP | 2. SERENITY | 3. QUIETED | 4. TRANQUIL | 5. STILLNESS | 6. RELAXATION
Mystery Answer: PLEASURE

194. GOD WILL SATISFY
Jumbles: 1. PIOUS | 2. PURITY | 3. WORTHWHILE | 4. DEVOUT | 5. VIRTUOUS | 6. REVERENCE
Mystery Answer: OUTSTRETCHED

195. GOD GIVES HIS HOLY SPIRIT
Jumbles: 1. BAPTISMAL | 2. CHRISTEN | 3. CEREMONY | 4. EUCHARIST | 5. IMMERSION | 6. SACRAMENT
Mystery Answer: TEMPTATION

196. GOD GIVES GRACE
Jumbles: 1. PARDON | 2. CHARITABLE | 3. LENIENCY | 4. REPRIEVE | 5. CLEMENCY | 6. COMPASSION
Mystery Answer: RECONCILIATION

197. GOD GIVES GOOD AND PERFECT GIFTS
Jumbles: 1. PREFERABLE | 2. FUNDING | 3. BOUNTIFUL | 4. AWARDED | 5. KEEPSAKE | 6. CONCESSION
Mystery Answer: BENEFACTOR

198. GOD GIVES HEALING AND SALVATION
Jumbles: 1. CURING | 2. HEALTH | 3. REMEDY | 4. NURSING | 5. HEALING | 6. WELLNESS
Mystery Answer: GENUINELY

199. GOD SHARES COMPLETE JOY
Jumbles: 1. BLISSFUL | 2. JUBILEE | 3. PLEASURE | 4. GLADNESS | 5. HAPPINESS | 6. MERRIMENT
Mystery Answer: LAUGHTER

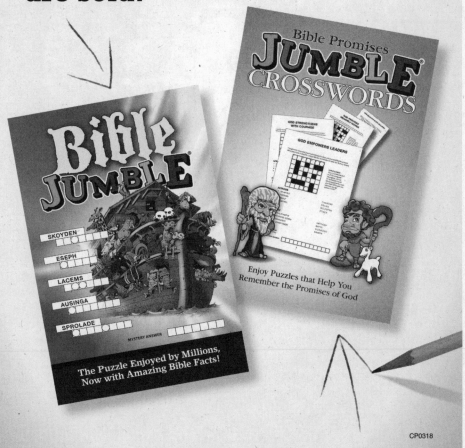